The War on Human Nature in Australia's Political Culture

Collected Essays

by Frank Salter

P.O. Box 4
Ourimbah NSW 2248
Australia

E-mail: f.salter@socialtechnologies.com.au

Dedicated to the memory of

Hiram Caton, 1936-2010.

Acknowledgements

The first five chapters are published with the permission of Quadrant magazine, in which they originally appeared under the following titles.

Chapter 1: (2012). "The war against human nature in the social sciences." Quadrant 56(6): 49-57.

Chapter 2: (2012). "The war against human nature II: Gender studies." Quadrant 56(7-8): 34-45.

Chapter 3: (2012). "The war against human nature III-1: Australia and the national question, part I: Race and the nation in the media." Quadrant 56(10): 66-73.

Chapter 4: (2012). "The war against human nature III-2: Australia and the national question, part II: Race and the nation in the universities." Quadrant 56(11): 36-44.

Chapter 5: Salter, F. K. (2010). "The misguided advocates of open borders." Quadrant 54(6).

The articles have been lightly edited to appear in the present volume.

The sixth chapter has not been published before. I thank Roger Masters and Wayne Hudson for helpful comments, Sonia Caton for her efforts in having Hiram's website restored at www.Hiram-Caton.com, which greatly facilitated this chapter, and Beya Aarts for providing valuable background information.

Table of Contents

Introduction to the Culture War on Human Nature

While lecturing in ex-Soviet countries from the 1990s it was difficult not to contrast the crumbling facades and rotten plumbing everywhere in evidence with neat Australian universities. There were two striking similarities—the vivid personalities who worked in both environments and the taboo against human nature afflicting the social sciences. Colleagues in Moscow, Novosibirsk, Prague, Budapest and Bucharest, recalled that during the communist era their attempts to adopt biosocial science—behavioural biology applied to the study of human society—were blocked by Marxists.[1] The discoveries of Charles Darwin, Konrad Lorenz, Nikko Tinbergen, William Young, Irenaeus Eibl-Eibesfeldt, William Hamilton, Edward Wilson and others were mainstream in the study of all species *except us*.

It felt just like home. An odd fact that: intolerant leftists held sway in universities on both sides of the Cold War. Ideas can be in poor repair in the best-funded universities.

---

[1]   One colleague explained how the Soviet authorities suppressed human ethology. New overseas developments in physics were immediately available, but he first learnt of Konrad Lorenz's book *On Aggression* ten years after it was written, and only then from a Russian translation of a book criticising Lorenz written by an Austrian Marxist.

The intellectual insularity of the social sciences was not a new theme. I had written about sociology's rejection of biology in a 1996 review of *The Concise Oxford Dictionary of Sociology*.[2] The *Dictionary* was embarrassingly true to the Standard Social Science Model that has been dominant since the 1930s, according to which the mind and behaviour are shaped only by culture. The *Dictionary* defined childhood, not as a critical stage of development that is genetically programmed and common to *Homo sapiens* everywhere, but as "constructed on the inabilities of children as political, intellectual, sexual, or economic beings, despite empirical evidence to the contrary. [This] serves the needs of capitalist states". The "Marriage" entry did not mention reproduction or child rearing. The entry under "Sex" denied the existence of instinctive sexuality. The "Race" entry denied that visible racial differences are the product of genes. There was no discussion of reproductive interests except for the usual mantra concerning social Darwinism, Herbert Spencer and eugenics. Many of these entries openly criticised conservative values, defining the latter so broadly as to include middle of the road values. There was no entry for "Patriotism". Just one biologically literate editor could have saved the book by informing contributors of the relevant biosocial facts.

The review's concluding words bear on the contemporary Australian scene: "Since evolutionary biology is a crucial artery linking the social and the natural sciences, closing off the free flow of biological ideas has resulted in the theoretical and empirical isolation evident in contemporary sociology as summarized in the *Dictionary*, and calls into question sociology's status as a science". I also noted that the part of biosocial science most relevant to understanding society consists of disciplines that study the naturalistic causes of social behaviour: ethology, sociobiology, evolutionary psychology,

---

2   Salter, F. K. (1996). "Sociology as alchemy [review of *The Concise Oxford Dictionary of Sociology*, 1994]." *Skeptic* 4(1): 50-59.

biological anthropology, biopolitics, bioeconomics, behavioural endocrinology, and brain science. Evolutionary theory is part of the tool kit of behavioural biology, useful for generating hypotheses about ultimate causes. All these approaches illuminate facets of human nature, especially those universal to the species.

The *Dictionary* was published almost two decades ago. The question I seek to answer here is whether behavioural biology is now a respectable part of Australia's elite culture. The question is important because many policy and management issues involve assessments of behaviour. Decision makers are unlikely to adopt prudent policies unless their reasoning is based on realistic assumptions about human nature. That applies whether one is trying to improve educational outcomes, increase the representation of women in non-domestic work roles, smooth race relations, or reduce bullying in schools and at work. To answer the question I shall consider three important domains of intellectual culture: the media, business, and academic social science.

Human nature in the media

On the positive side behavioural biology comes up frequently in the media, probably due to consumer demand. We are living at an exciting time of discovery in the field. The human genome was decoded in 2003 resulting in a steady trickle of news about gene expression. At the same time other species' genomes are being decoded, most recently that of the gorilla, allowing insights into human adaptations.

Many articles are syndicated from Europe or the United States, but Australian researchers are represented. Rob Brooks, professor of evolutionary biology at the University of NSW, recently published *Sex, Genes & Rock 'n' Roll: How Evolution Has Shaped the Modern World*, described by the *Sydney*

Morning Herald as a "sublime piece of popular science". Brooks applies modern evolutionary theory to understand sex and sexuality. On Valentine's Day he discussed how even romantic relationships must overcome the competitiveness and aggression that is normal, especially between unrelated individuals. The heavy lifting is performed by the hormones oxytocin and vasopressin.[3]

Melbourne University sociologist Ruth Quibell's review of *The Conflict: Woman and Mother* by French feminist Elisabeth Badinter raises doubts about the latter's opposition to naturalistic mothering.[4] Badinter argues that sociobiological theory is being used by "reactionaries" to shame mothers into putting their careers on hold in order to prioritise baby care. Quibell agrees with Badinter that breast feeding, co-sleeping and intervention-free birthing do make parenting more difficult. But Quibell thinks that women are capable of choosing between full-time careers and children. "[Badinter's] nostalgia for carefree smoking and drinking while pregnant seems less a lament for lost feminine freedoms and more a defence of retrograde hedonism."

There is a stream of related articles, as indicated by these snapshots. Ross Gittins, a leading business journalist with the *Sydney Morning Herald*, favourably reviewed a U.S. book that argues for economic regulation based on Darwinian theory.[5] Articles on self improvement are becoming better informed and realistic in their claims: "Genetics matter but there's still much you can do to obtain the body you want . . .".[6] Numerous stories about performance-enhancing drugs in sport mention the

---

3   "The Course of True Love Was Never about Profit", *SMH* 14 Feb. 2012, p. 11.

4   *SMH* 4-5 Feb. 2012, Spectrum, p. 35.

5   *SMH* 23-25 Dec. 2011, Weekend Business p. 8. The book is Robert Frank's, *The Darwin Economy*.

6   *Sun Herald* 11 March 2012, p. 20.

biochemistry of growth and sex differences. That testosterone produces masculine appearance and behaviour is perhaps the best reported fact about behavioural biology. A recent discussion of the emotion of disgust—its brain centres, expression and functions—was reprinted in *The Sun Herald*[7] from *The New York Times*. Medical genetics is well represented. An article on the disadvantages of Attention Deficit Hyperactivity Disorder reported its genetic basis and its concentration in boys and men.

Contemporary criticisms of biosocial science are less radical than the absolute denials of 1970s and 1980s. An example is a full-page feature article critical of evolutionary psychology in the *Weekend Australian*[8] by a Californian psychologist. In its discussion of adolescence the article conceded: "One of the most distinctive evolutionary features of human beings is our unusually long, protected childhood. Human children depend on adults for much longer than those of any other primate." Both sides of this debate have adopted some of the same evolutionary premises.

There is strong demand for natural history television programmes, such as David Attenborough's BBC productions. The latest exotic skull from the human past can be front page news, with information about the lost species' diet, range and competitive challenges. For example, *Sydney Morning Herald* readers were recently informed about a previously unknown extinct population of hominids found to have lived in China.[9] The report noted that an Australian researcher helped make the find, that it had primitive features such as a thick skull but also the imprint of modern frontal lobes, that the population had survived until 11,500 years ago, and that it did not interbreed

---

7   *Sun Herald*, 29 Jan. 2012, Extra, p. 4.

8   Alison Gopnik, *The Weekend Australian*, 11-12 Feb. 2012, Inquirer, p. 17.

9   *SMH*, 15 March 2012, p. 1.

with modern humans. Such reports inject evolutionary perspectives into popular culture. An American television documentary[10] shown on SBS TV discussed *Homo erectus*. The program explained that the species was the most successful of human ancestors, not as measured by lifestyle or health but because it survived for two million years, an acknowledgement of long-term perspectives and group continuity in an era of instant gratification and hyper-individualism.

Another British documentary aired on ABC TV examined the subject of human intelligence.[11] There has been much controversy and vituperation on this aspect of human behaviour, both when it involves comparison of races or comparison of classes within the one ethnic group. The program informed viewers that the IQ test is still the most common measure of intelligence but that IQ tells only "half the story". Other intelligence tests were discussed and it was noted that psychologists could not agree on how to improve on IQ. Biological factors were downplayed, such as IQ's strong heritability. Also not mentioned was that IQ, despite limitations, is a powerful predictor of educational achievement and social mobility.[12]

A more forthright discussion of intelligence and society is economics Professor Judith Sloan's review of *Coming Apart: The State of White America, 1960-2010*, the new book by political scientist Charles Murray.[13] Murray's book is an empirical confirmation of the thesis advanced in his *The Bell*

---

[10]   SBS One, Lost Worlds, WGBH production, 11 March 2012.

[11]   "Battle of the Brains", ABC1 TV, 27 Feb. 2012, produced for Horizon by the BBC in 2007.

[12]   Salter, F. K. (2008). Class mobility, environment, and genes: A Darwinian conflict analysis. In *The new evolutionary social science: Human nature, social behavior, and social change*. Edited by H.-J. Niedenzu, T. Meleghy and P. Meyer. Boulder, Colorado, Paradigm: 159-171.

[13]   Judith Sloan, in *The Weekend Australian*, 17-18 March 2012, Inquirer, p. 17.

Curve, the bestselling tome of 1994 that he co-authored with psychologist Richard Herrnstein. That earlier book was strongly criticised on ideological grounds, though its premises concerning IQ and educational performance are widely accepted among cognitive psychologists. It argued that a self-perpetuating cognitive elite is developing in the United States due to the ongoing segregation and intermarriage of professionals in top universities and exclusive neighbourhoods. Sloan manages to avoid the terms "IQ", "intelligence" and "bell curve" but gets the message across with terms such as "exceptional intellectual ability" and "highest cognitive abilities". It has long been known that higher education is stratified. Murray shows how far this has gone. The pinnacle of the system comprises a score of elite universities such as Harvard and Princeton, which are gatekeepers to the high income professions. And because spouses tend to meet one another at university or work ("educational homogamy" in Murray's terminology), the IQ advantage is passed onto children more reliably than it was in the past. The cognitive-economic elite has arrived, at least in the U.S. Hopefully Sloan is correct in her assessment that Australia's elite is lagging behind America's in that regard. A newspaper review cannot be exhaustive and Sloan does not mention that a necessary part of Murray's overall analysis is that when gross inequalities in nutrition are reduced, differences in intelligence result largely from genetic variation. Nor is research noted showing that IQ predicts much social mobility. In his new book Murray himself does not report cross-disciplinary research by Richard Lynn and Tatu Vanhanen showing that average national IQ correlates strongly with GDP. The finding indicates that China, freed of the most debilitating constraints of communism, has a long way to go before its economic growth levels off.[14] The review is a refreshing reminder of how biosocial science can help unpick

---

[14]   Lynn, R. and T. Vanhanen (2002). *IQ and the wealth of nations*. Westport, Conn., Praeger.

complex social phenomena, such as patterns of social mobility within and between populations.

Geneticists studying intelligence are beginning to identify the many genes contributing to brain function. On 16 April 2012 an understated news item on the ABC website reported a major breakthrough, partly led by two Australian geneticists, Nick Martin and Margaret Wright at the Queensland Institute for Medical Research. This was the largest brain study ever undertaken, involving over 20,000 subjects and 200 scientists. The research, involving brain scans, genetic epidemiology, and IQ testing, found a gene that codes for a small fraction of brain size and IQ.[15]

The educated public has become aware of biosocial themes thanks to media reports such as those described above. That awareness is assumed by commentators and humorists, allowing hyperbole and levity to be predicated upon it. For example, Richard Glover of the *Sydney Morning Herald* writes: "[Men] see a woman, a woman of appropriate age, and in our ears a heavenly choir begins to sing. The whole weight of evolution bears down on us; the history of the planet itself; our DNA thrums with one question: 'Could this be the opportunity I have long sought to fulfil my genetic destiny and to go forth and multiply, albeit in the nicest, consensual, mutually pleasurable way.'"[16]

Any discussion of evolutionary themes in the media must include the omnipresent atheist Richard Dawkins. His latest appearance was on the ABC's *Q&A* on 9th April, debating Cardinal George Pell, the Catholic Archbishop of Sydney, on whether the universe had a creator. Dawkins is an emeritus fellow of Oxford University. For much of his career he has been an influential public educator on how the myriad adaptations

---

[15]   *http://www.abc.net.au/science/articles/2012/04/16/3478267.htm*

[16]   Richard Glover, *SMH*, 3-4 March 2012, Spectrum p. 5.

found in the natural world are produced by natural selection. His first great publishing success, *The Selfish Gene* (1976), sold over a million copies in 25 languages. The ideas and prose were captivating, though I agree with the author that a more appropriate title would have been *The Altruistic Gene*.

Dawkins has a genius for slicing and dicing the indigestible mathematics of Darwinian theory into metaphorical titbits. He has attained celebrity status, appearing with other luminaries where gravitas and clear diction are needed. But Dawkins' contribution to injecting biosocial science into public debates is limited and not always positive. Certainly his views concerning natural selection help clear away obfuscation[17] but they introduce others.[18] Dawkins made it clear decades ago that he does not challenge biological illiteracy in the social sciences. In some respects he resembles the Marxist critics of sociobiology who praise evolution for its atheistic implications while opposing any use of biology to analyse society. Biosocial science has been advanced by scholars of all political persuasions. But its most powerful enemies have not been theists but left ideologues, including grandiloquent Darwinians such as Richard Lewontin and the late Stephen Jay Gould. Given this background, Dawkins' proselytising atheism could well be retarding the spread of evolutionary ideas by reinforcing the false impression that Darwinism is necessarily hostile to religion and the middle ground of political values. It is disappointing that he has focused his energies on attacking a target that is soft by virtue of lying outside science. The mismatch, which at times resembles blood sport, would be less jarring if he took on the hardened irrationalism of the social sciences.

---

[17] See Richard Dawkins interview Steven Rose:
   http://www.dailymotion.com/video/xdvj1r_steven-rose_tech

[18] Salter, F. K. (2008). "Misunderstandings of kin selection and the delay in quantifying ethnic kinship." *Mankind Quarterly* 48(3): 311-344.

A truer champion of biology in the social sciences is Harvard linguist Steven Pinker, whose books such as *How the Mind Works* and *The Blank Slate: The Modern Denial of Human Nature* have helped popularise evolutionary psychology. Unlike Dawkins, Pinker has taken on biological denialism in the social sciences. He has criticised the intolerance usually directed at biosocial scientists when they breach socialist taboos. His new book, *The Better Angels of Our Nature: The Decline of Violence in History and Its Causes* was reviewed twice in the *Sydney Morning Herald*. One review, by Macquarie University law professor Frank Carrigan, had a highlighted sentence: "Humans were wired for violence from the outset." The review included trenchant criticism but judged the book to be "brilliantly conceived".[19] In the other review, international editor Peter Hartcher related Pinker's thesis to contemporary warfare and the rise of China.[20]

Inevitably the science of human nature is entering the political culture, even if it must often bypass social scientists and disengaged biologists to do so. Popularisation is no substitute for academic analysis. But it can whet curiosity. As biosocial science opens beachheads in the United States and Europe, Australian gatekeepers will find it more difficult to police the culture. Meanwhile, biobehavioural information is largely absent from political editorials and analyses by leading political correspondents. When it does appear in the media it concerns relatively uncontroversial subjects. Biosocial science is limited to gossip and mostly kept away from the serious business of debating policy.

---

[19]   Frank Carrigan, *SMH Review*, 18-19 Feb. 2012, pp. 18-19.

[20]   Peter Hartcher, *SMH*, 31 Jan. 2012, p. 11.

Human nature in business culture

Although MBA courses in Australia's management schools do not yet include findings from behavioural biology, executive coaching programs sometimes allow that input. Management culture and the consultancy industry have been more open to ideas coming from ethology and evolutionary psychology than the social sciences.

Andrew O'Keeffe, a well-respected senior human resources consultant based in Sydney, deploys findings from primatology and evolutionary psychology to coach business leaders and help businesses cope with organisational change. He is the author of *Hardwired Humans: Successful Leadership Using Human Instincts* (Roundtable, 2011). O'Keeffe adapts research by biosocial scientists such as Nigel Nicholson, a professor of organisational behaviour at the London Business School. This research is integrated with findings from evolutionary biology, for example the primatology of Jane Goodall and the anthropology of Robin Dunbar.

Human nature has long figured in popular ideas about management. In 1971 Antony Jay wrote a popular book applying ethology to modern management before using its insights to co-author the *Yes Minister* series for the BBC. One can almost smell cabinet intrigues in the book title: *Corporation Man; Who He Is, What He Does, Why His Ancient Tribal Impulses Dominate the Life of the Modern Corporation*. Jay—now Sir Antony Jay—is still applying those insights to current events. Recently he analysed the BBC's persistent leftist bias in terms that could be applied to our ABC or the social science establishment.

Anyone familiar with large organisations knows that over the years they develop and perpetuate their own ethos, their own value system, their own corporate beliefs and standards. . . . Those at the top of the tree are the custodians of corporate orthodoxy; they recruit applicants in their own image, and the applicants are steadily indoctrinated with the organisation's principles and practices. Heretics tend to leave fairly early in their careers (London *Telegraph*, 10 Dec. 2011).[21]

Ethology's emphasis on non-verbal behaviour ("body language") makes it a good fit for analysing and coaching managers. Some graduates of ethology courses have been doing business as management consultants since the 1980s, initially in the United States and more recently in Germany. Bio-behavioural research into business behaviour is most advanced in the United States and Britain. Relevant fields are human resources and marketing. A recent example is a study into race relations and discrimination. The research employed functional magnetic resonance imaging to view brain activity while subjects made decisions about inter-ethnic behaviour. The study was led by Michael Norton, Associate Professor of Business Administration in the Marketing Unit at the Harvard Business School, previously at MIT's Sloan School of Management.[22]

The likely cause of business being more open to human nature is the unforgiving nature of economic competition. The churning of businesses and the spilling of red ink bear a resemblance to nature in tooth and claw. The constant winnowing of careers and firms keeps existential realities before business leaders' eyes, a tonic for the ideology-afflicted. Another likely factor is the connection with economics. Economic theories must sooner or later work in the real world, which arguably keeps them on a shorter empirical leash than sociological and anthropological theories.

---

[21]   *http://blogs.telegraph.co.uk/news/jamesdelingpole/100123173/sir-antony-jay-slash-the-bbc-by-two-thirds/*

[22]   Norton, M. I., M. F. Mason, et al. (2012). "An fMRI investigation of racial paralysis." *Social Cognition and Affective Neuroscience.*

Human nature in the social sciences

Biosocial theories considered highly problematic and even repugnant in Australian social science are accepted in a growing number of universities overseas, especially in the United States.

Around 1980 Australian social science fitted a general pattern of excluding human nature from teaching and research. Marx and Weber were in. Darwin was out. That situation had its origins near the start of the 20th century, when radical ideology began to come into fashion among American intellectuals. A politically inspired movement developed in the United States that worked to marginalise the concept of human nature in the social sciences. The task was considerable because the founders of anthropology and sociology, such as William Sumner and Edward Ross, knew that human nature was important. How that movement grew and maintained its hermeneutic intolerance is properly the subject for another essay, though there is already a considerable literature on the subject.[23] By the 1940s behavioural biology was indeed marginalised in the social sciences in the United States. Its lowly status was spread afar when the university system expanded after the Second World War and the United States became the powerhouse of social science research by mid century. Human nature began its return slowly in the 1970s, a trend that continues.

In the early 21st century, biosocial science is a growing and influential trend in American anthropology and psychology, with a smaller though well-established presence in political science. Even in sociology the bio-behavioural approach has a presence, though the ideological headwinds are strongest in that discipline.

---

[23] Degler, C. (1991). *In search of human nature: The decline and revival of Darwinism in American social thought.* Oxford, Oxford University Press. Segerstråle, U. (2000). Defenders of truth: The battle for science in the sociobiology debate and beyond. New York, Oxford University Press. Kaufmann, E. (2004). *The rise and fall of Anglo-America.* Cambridge, MA, Harvard University Press.

A comparable history of the Australian academic scene has not been attempted. However, some evidence is available. First an anecdote. During my experience as a student of political science from the late 1970s through to 1990 at the University of Sydney and Griffith University in Brisbane, I came across only one scholar who systematically applied behavioural biology to social science analysis. Hiram Caton (1936-2010) supervised my masters and doctoral research at Griffith, both in the interdisciplinary field of biosocial science. In 1988 we published a bibliography of the field[24] and updated it in 1993.[25] During those years behavioural biology was marginal in Australian social science.

At the end of the century Caton took stock of Australian biopolitics in an article appropriately titled "'Biopolitics? Never heard of it': A report from Australia".[26] Despite the title, the article dealt with "all research involving synthesis between social and biological sciences". Caton circulated a survey to 31 persons, receiving 18 responses. He also searched nine university websites for biosocial content of curricula and government websites concerned with higher education policy. This was a formal update of a previous assessment he made in a 1982 paper.[27] In neither paper could he report significant uptake of behavioural biology in Australian social sciences. He himself abandoned attempts to teach the subject in the 1990s due to pressure from colleagues.

---

[24] Caton, H. P. and F. K. Salter (1988). *A bibliography of biosocial science*. Brisbane, St. Albans Press.

[25] Caton, H. P., F. K. Salter, and J. van der Dennen (1993). *The bibliography of human behavior*. Westport, Conn., Greenwood Press.

[26] Caton, H. P. (2001). 'Biopolitics? Never heard of it': A report from Australia. *Evolutionary approaches in the behavioral sciences: Toward a better understanding of human nature*. S. A. Peterson and A. Somit. Amsterdam, JAI-Elsevier Science: 247-269.

[27] Caton, H. P. (1982). *Biosocial science: Knowledge for enlightened political leadership*. Paper prepared for the American Political Science Association annual convention, Denver, Colorado, 2-6 September.

All except two of Caton's respondents agreed with his questionnaire's assumption that "there was something odd or dysfunctional about the failure of biobehavioral research to develop in Australia" (p. 250). One unnamed critic disagreed with biosocial science on the mistaken assumption that it consisted of sociobiological theory. The latter was in fact only one strand of the biosocial conceptual tool kit, which also includes ethology, endocrinology, and social technology theory. The other, zoologist S. A. (Tony) Barnett (1915-2003), also opposed sociobiology but in addition opposed the notion of a fixed human nature.

Barnett's views warrant discussion because of his influential stance against biosocial science in Australia in the 1970s and 1980s. His influence was partly due to his prestige as a professor of zoology at the Australian National University. In addition he was frequently provided a platform by ABC Radio, a gate keeper of high culture in Australia.[28]

Caton had known Barnett personally since the 1970s and agreed with his criticism of Darwinians' overconfidence. Caton rejected as presumptious the notion that anthropology, sociology and political science could be branches of biology, that sociobiology could somehow preempt social science.[29] He saw biobehavioural analysis as a necessary but far from sufficient foundation. At the same time he thought it unreasonable to exclude behavioural biology from social science curricula. It was from this perspective that Caton wrote with authority in 2001 that "[f]or nearly four decades he [Barnett] has, as science publicist and author, discouraged the birth of the dreaded hybrid [biosocial science]." Barnett spoke with passion against any attempts to apply Darwinian theory to the study of human society partly on

---

[28] On the ABC's *The Science Show* and *Ockham's Razor* (*http://currawong.net/s-a-barnett/*)

[29] Rosenberg, A. (1981). *Sociobiology and the preemption of social science*. Baltimore, Johns Hopkins University Press.

scientific grounds but also because it would, he thought, restrict freedom, dignity and autonomy. He opposed biology-based ideas about human nature because they reinforced pessimistic stereotypes of humans as selfish, violent, mendacious, sexually opportunistic, competitive and exploitative. Barnett thought that future society could be free of such behaviours and opposed any ideas—such as that of an innate human nature—likely to weaken society's resolve to abolish them. Caton raised the obvious objection that all of these traits are "empirically quite pronounced" and, moreover, consistent with Darwinian theory. Acknowledging them as part of human nature is not pessimistic but realistic, so why not accept the observations and abandon utopia?

Caton implied that Barnett's absolute rejection of biosocial science did not follow from scientific arguments. It was politically motivated, especially regarding issues of race. His publications on the subject show that his historical arguments were derived from the left establishment in the United States, including discredited founders such as Franz Boas and his school.[30] Another resemblance was Barnett's hostility to the Western tradition when it inevitably contradicted his utopianism. He characterised neo-Darwinian images of humanity as "emphasising human depravity". "In their misanthropy they reflect the outlook of conservative pessimists who have influenced European thought for two and a half millennia. . .".[31]

Like the Marxist critics Stephen J. Gould and Richard Lewontin, Barnett did not fully acknowledge that the extreme selectionist models at the heart of the project were not ends in themselves but hypotheses to be tested and modified in light of

---

[30] See the references on race in Barnett, S. A. (1988). *Biology and freedom: An essay on the implications of human ethology.* Cambridge, Cambridge University Press.

[31] Barnett, S. A. (1983). "Humanity and natural selection." *Ethology and Sociobiology* 4(1): 35-51, p. 35.

data.[32] A theory is valuable if, despite oversimplification, it inspires cycles of hypothesising, testing, and theoretical revision. Barnett's position was more subtle than that of Gould and Lewontin. His discussion of mathematical biology showed an appreciation of how simplified models contribute to knowledge. However, he did not credit the advances made by selectionist models as heuristics in studying human social behaviour.

The case of Richard Dawkins' offensive against the Church discussed earlier suggests that Barnett was too worried about neo-Darwinism violating leftist taboos. For generations Darwinism has been used selectively to attack religion—mainly Christianity—but not applied to anti-biological irrationalism in academe.

At the turn of the 21st century Caton's survey found political pressure from that direction to be a major retardant of biosocial science. He cited an example of graduate students in anthropology stating that their supervisors "warned them not to get involved with evolutionary perspectives because of the political dangers to their careers". More about political bias presently.

In March 2011, to survey the place of biosocial science in Australia, I wrote to 31 deans and professors in university departments of politics, anthropology, and sociology. I asked them for information about "the status of and prospects for biosocial courses or research" in their departments.[33] The letter defined biosocial science broadly as "the study of political and social phenomena using knowledge, methods and theory drawn from behavioural biology", and concluded: "Is biosocial science

---

[32] Barnett, S. A. (1988). *Biology and freedom: An essay on the implications of human ethology*. Cambridge, Cambridge University Press, pp. 91-3.

[33] This number was coincidentally the same as Caton's.

taught in [the department] or are there plans to do so? If not, what do you think are the prospects of introducing it?"

There were eighteen responses from fifteen departments situated in nine universities. Several respondents found my description of biosocial science interesting and regretted that their department did not teach it or plan to. However, all except one response were variations on this succinct reply: "The short answer to your question is: no, and no." The one partial exception was the School of Archaeology and Anthropology at the Australian National University. A professor wrote that the answer to my question depended on how "biosocial science" was defined. If it meant "aspects of human life in which social and biological processes play interacting roles" then "quite a few of our courses have a biosocial theme running through them". The topics were treated by the *Journal of Biosocial Science*.[34] However he thought that I meant specific theories. In that sense, the most relevant course in the School examined controversies surrounding theories that treated human societies as animal societies. Those theories included ethology, sociobiology, behavioural ecology, and evolutionary psychology. Thus even this one exception did not deploy behavioural biology to study society or train students how to do so. Instead it examined controversies that arose from such deployment.

The stance against biosocial science has not been absolute. Caton recalled ANU anthropologist Derek Freeman's drawing on ethology in his 1983 criticism of Margaret Mead's book on Samoa. While head of his department, Freeman recruited a researcher on nonverbal behaviour. Biologists outside the social sciences continue to do research relevant to behaviour and every now and then comment on social implications. A high-profile example was Nobel Prize laureate Macfarlane Burnet (1899-1985) who, though an immunologist, ventured into the subject of social power. In *The Endurance of Life: The*

---

[34]   *http://journals.cambridge.org/action/displayJournal?jid=JBS*

Implications of Genetics for Human Life (1978), Burnet dealt mainly with ageing. But he also discussed behaviour and power, demonstrating familiarity with the ethology and sociobiology of the time. Burnet was publicly criticised for giving a "dismal, unappealing view of humanity".

Away from such controversies Australian scientists have been building expertise in such fields as behaviour genetics, neuroscience, behavioural economics, and animal behavioural ecology. The last is the lineal descendant of Edward O. Wilson's sociobiology. These disciplines study biological aspects of behaviour, emphasising individual and group differences and reproductive strategies. Rob Brooks, the behavioural ecologist from UNSW discussed earlier, began studying life history strategies in fish, insects and mice in Johannesburg and found that the same biological principles applied to human *Sex & Rock 'n' Roll*. Other prominent Australian biosocial scientists, mentioned earlier, are Nick Martin and Margaret Wright at the Genetic Epidemiology Laboratory in Brisbane. Martin is a leading twin researcher who helped establish the Australian twin register in 1978. Housed at the Queensland Institute for Medical Research, the registry has grown to be one of the world's largest repositories of twin data. Martin and Wright helped initiate the Enigma Consortium, a cooperative venture by over 200 scientists that recently achieved a breakthrough in identifying the first "intelligence gene". The gene accounts for 1% of differences in IQ. One of Martin and Wright's contributions was to show that brain size correlates with IQ. The study has relevance to understanding ageing and dementia as well as the structure and development of intelligence.

It is the rise of evolutionary psychology that poses the greatest threat to the disciplinary isolation of the social sciences. The new field emerged from sociobiology in the 1980s in journals such as *Ethology and Sociobiology* (now *Evolution and Human Behavior*) and *Behavioral and Brain Sciences*. Since then graduate students have fed back into psychology departments and others have found utility in theories such as domain-specific cognition, slow and fast life history strategies, genetic similarity, parental investment, and models of selection. Psychology is a bridging discipline that helps introduce behavioural science into studies of society, for example via the interdisciplinary field of political psychology. It will be interesting to watch whether this new trend, together with other branches of behavioural biology, increases the pressure on the social science perimeter.

The emergence of evolutionary psychology returns the discipline to its biological roots, with a revival of interest in physiology and adaptive behaviour in natural settings. It also represents the revenge of sociobiology. Evolutionary psychology developed from the ferment of ideas and research ignited by one of the greatest scientific controversies of the last century. It began in 1975 when Harvard University professor Edward O. Wilson included a chapter on humans in his magisterial opus *Sociobiology: The New Synthesis,* which brought together current theory and data on animal social behaviour. The central theoretical problem was altruism, which is held by utopians to be something owed by all to all, but which in fact is channelled disproportionately towards kin in all animals species. Wilson came under furious assault from Marxist vigilantes who perceived a challenge to their academic hegemony.[35] Leading lights such as Richard Lewontin and Steven Rose led the charge. They rejected the validity of behavioural genetics as a whole, which underlay Martin and Wright's discovery of a gene for brain size described above. Wilson fought back with books such as *On Human Nature* (1978) and *Genes, Mind, and Culture* (1981), which pioneered the theory of gene-culture

---

[35] Wilson, E. O. (1978). Academic vigilantism and the political significance of sociobiology. *The sociobiology debate: Readings on the ethical and scientific issues concerning sociobiology.* A. L. Caplan. New York, Harper and Row: 291-303.

evolution. In *Consilience* (1998) Wilson advocated unifying knowledge from biology, the humanities and the social sciences.

Wilson lost the battle in the sense that the social sciences did not embrace sociobiology. In the social sciences and humanities the term came to represent dangerous reactionism (i.e. middle of the road conservatism). The term "sociobiology" was successfully stigmatised and was dropped even by many practitioners. However, it seems that Wilson is winning the war because many psychologists (and in the U.S. anthropologists) are working again on human nature and explicitly drawing on biobehavioural data and methods. In Australia, several respondents reported taking up this type of research on its merits, not due to overseas connections. This corroborates the impression of the artificiality and growing fragility of the social sciences' taboo against biology.

Recently the American social psychologist Jonathan Haidt described how the social sciences reproduce their intolerant political agenda. Like Antony Jay and the BBC, Haidt knows his subject from the inside. Indeed, he presented his criticisms at the annual meeting of the Society for Personality and Social Psychology, in January 2011.[36] Haidt argued that the discipline of social psychology is a "tribal-moral society" that shuts out research and researchers likely to produce results that conflict with liberal (i.e. socialist) beliefs.

Haidt based this thesis on three observations. First, social psychologists have sacred values that are neither empirical nor methodological dogmas. These values take the form of taboos that constrain thinking. Secondly, they have created a homogeneous society. There is almost no moral or political diversity within the discipline. While conservatives outnumber liberals 2-to-1 in the general U.S. population, they are

---

[36]   Jonathan Haidt, "The bright future of post-partisan social psychology", 27 Jan. 2011, *http://www.authorstream.com/Presentation/jhaidt-819710-haidt-postpartisan-social-psychology/*

outnumbered 200 or 300-to-1 within social psychology. Haidt managed to locate only one declared conservative social psychology academic. Finally, social psychologists have created a hostile environment that suppresses and discourages non-liberals, such as libertarians and conservatives. He gave examples of how conservative students are intimidated into not pursuing social psychology for fear of the social environment in the discipline and the taboo-breaking results they might find. The situation described by Haidt is a microcosm of the soft totalitarianism that a radicalised intellectual elite has imposed on Western societies since the Second World War.

The taboos identified by Haidt concern race and sex differences, blaming the victim, stereotype accuracy, and nativism. The lack of political diversity hurts the discipline because different points of view lead to the discovery of novel phenomena. What Haidt found in social psychology also exists in the liberal social sciences. Haidt's report agrees with Hiram Caton's article discussed earlier about the importance of political correctness in selecting personnel in the social sciences and how it shapes research agendas and chills creativity from student times onwards.

Despite promising signs, until now Australian social sciences have managed to keep human nature at bay. While not monolithic, the exclusion of biosocial science has been effective enough to retain the Standard Social Science Model as the accepted dogma in many departments. The situation is a harsher version of that overseas. Disciplines whose subject is human social behaviour generally do not include biological information in their curricula or research. It is like economists considering money to be unmentionable or physicists writing off certain particles for lack of charm.

Behavioural biology is making headway in psychology while the sociological disciplines—sociology, anthropology and political science together with specialist areas such as gender studies—have maintained the rage against any science that dispels utopian dreams. The result has been the unfolding, largely unwitting, of the Gramscian vision of training a new intellectual elite, year after year, generation after generation. That is how the social sciences long ago became a vital area of strength for leftist hegemony in Western intellectual culture and a breeding ground for radical movements.

Conclusion

The social sciences' stand against behavioural biology is leaving them increasingly isolated and irrelevant. News about human nature attracts audiences and as a result is opening up popular culture to information more advanced than that made available university courses. Business often sees the relevance of hardwired social behaviour to management practice. Behavioural biology's influence in adjacent disciplines such as psychology and economics is growing. The social science role of providing analysis and social technologies for governments and corporations is being poached by disciplines that are less ideologically and theoretically constrained.

My personal experience illustrates the contrast between the popular, business and academic taste for the science of human nature. During postgraduate research in biosocial science at Griffith University, from 1984 to 1990, non-academics would often express interest in the subject. I remember conversations about human universals, body language, evolutionary history, biological sex differences, sexual identity, power, ethnicity, child behaviour, and so on. The same interest frequently came from academics not immersed in the social sciences. In 1990 the local ABC radio station sensed that interest and invited me to present a few talkback sessions on body language. Managers also expressed interest. Two federal bureaucracies engaged me to detect and prevent occupational stress. But the academic response in the social sciences was weak or antagonistic. Over the next twenty years I experienced a slow warming of attitudes by social scientists in Europe and the United States, and frequent enthusiasm among students. The survey described above indicates a growing latent interest in biosocial science but it has not yet found practical expression in teaching and research.

A caveat is in order concerning the foregoing review, which has not been exhaustive. It is possible that sociology students somewhere are being introduced to behavioural endocrinology or that political science students are learning about primate social models and field observational methods. At the same time it should be emphasised that my criticisms of social science concern lack of pluralism, and is not directed at whole fields of knowledge. Biosocial science can aspire only to being an aspect of these disciplines.

At the start of this chapter I suggested that just one biologically informed editor could have saved *The Concise Oxford Dictionary of Sociology*. The same applies to departments of sociology, anthropology and political science in Australian universities. A light seasoning of colleagues whose research draws on the biological sciences would give departmental cultures a taste of the natural world. That would be interdisciplinarity with teeth. Who knows? It might hasten the end of the Gramscian assault on human nature.

What to do about our universities? At this juncture, after such a negative review, readers might expect me to suggest remedies. Apart from a policy of waiting for the inevitable, I do not pretend to know them. More important at this stage is to assess the damage done to our political culture by over half a century of tribal-moral social science. That is the task of future chapters.

Sexless Gender Studies

In the previous chapter I described the isolation of Australian social sciences from behavioural biology and suggested that this weakness had given free rein to utopian ideologies. Human nature is slow to change. It a conservative force. As such it is an obstacle for ideologues wishing transformational social change. The last thing a utopian wants to discuss is how society reflects human instincts. Better to avoid the subject altogether to create a parallel universe where imagination, passion and interests might collude. In this chapter I extend this thesis to gender studies with emphasis on women and work.

Gender is an obvious choice of subject for testing the acceptance of biology in the social sciences because the differences between men and women are known to have a strong biological component (more of which presently). And gender relations are increasingly important within work organisations. The trickle of women into extra-household work roles has become a flood. Women often outnumber men in work categories, including as university graduates entering the workforce. Work relations between unrelated men and women have become a normal part of life, intensifying issues of equal opportunity, discrimination, sexuality and rank, and female leadership. This has resulted from women having unprecedented freedom of life-styles, though choices still inflict tradeoffs, most notably between career and children. Does the advice given to citizens, government, and business take human nature into account? At the end of this chapter I discuss some biological aspects of gender and work, concerning dominance relations between men and women. Before doing so it is necessary to size up the amount of behavioural biology in the media's coverage of gender, in university gender studies programs, and in philosopher Simone de Beavoir's classic formulation of women as eternal victims.

Gender in the media

The media are a useful place to begin assessing the understanding of gender in public culture. The media influence public perceptions by filtering information and helping to set the limits the legitimate discussion. Unopposed criticism of ideas or social categories (sex, age, ethnicity etc.) sends powerful messages to the public about the relative standing of ideologies and interest groups. Media content also reveals the information being received from various experts – the universities, government, and political activists.

Media reports and commentaries concerning gender and work address several themes.

Reports of behavioural research findings. There is a trickle of these reports, a recent example being an American study that found a preference among voters, male and female, for politicians with lower-pitched voices. The authors speculated that this could explain some of the underrepresentation of women in elected office.[37] Bettina Arndt is an Australian analyst who has included biological factors in her discussions of sexuality since the 1970s. Her most recent book, *What Men Want* (2010, chapters 3 and 4), is based on interviews and

---

[37] *http://www.theage.com.au/national/bobs-booming-voice-could-be-election-winner-20120314-1uzfr.html*, accessed 18 May 2012.

refers to research in evolutionary psychology, neuroscience, and sexual physiology. In a recent article Arndt discussed women's tactics in attracting men, such as dressing to show breasts.[38] Her story, appropriately titled "Busted: the politics of cleavage and a glance" combined anecdote, interviews and behavioural science. She drew on research on male-female differences in sex drive to argue that women who dress sexily in public are flaunting their sexual power and running risks. The results can be unpleasant. Another article was titled "Why successful women lose the dating game".[39] Arndt reports that in 2006 many Australian women lacked partners: almost a third aged 30-34 and a quarter in their late 30s. This was almost double the 1986 figures. A contributing factor was women's preference for similarly qualified men combined with demographics. In 2006 there were 88,000 single degreed women in their thirties but only 68,000 unattached degreed men in the same age group. "The 30s are worrying years for high-achieving women who long for marriage and children – of course, not all do – as they face their rapidly closing reproductive window surrounded by men who see no rush to settle down."

Arndt's articles attracted criticism for allegedly exonerating sexism and misogyny. She has come under fire from the gender studies movement for the same reason. One columnist[40] disagreed with Arndt's blaming the sexual signals emitted by women and not men's failure to control their behaviour. Only men are to blame for their bad behaviour towards women because men should "grasp the concept that looking sexy doesn't necessarily make you sexually available". The two parties talked somewhat past one another, Arndt focusing on

---

[38] Bettina Arndt, "Busted: The politics of cleavage and a glance", *Sun-Herald*, Extra, 12 Feb. 2012, pp. 1-3.

[39] Bettina Arndt, "Why successful women lose the dating game", *Sun-Herald*, Extra, 22 April 2012, pp. 86-7.

[40] Josephine Tovey, "Low expectations, not necklines, to blame for misogyny", *Sydney Morning Herald*, 15 Feb. 2002, p. 13.

cause and effect, Tovey on morality. Both sides of the exchange made good points, but confirmed Arndt's premise that many young women hold to the expectation that their sexual behaviour, including sexual displays, will not have evil consequences because they should not.

Female disability. This is a common type of gender story, usually alleging the unfair underrepresentation of women in an occupation or role, such as blue collar jobs and executive and board positions in business. A related focus is causes of female underrepresentation, such as male discrimination, stereotypes, and inadequate child care. This category also includes reports of sexual harassment suffered at work, such as the spate of trials of male naval officers charged with harassing female shipmates.[41]

Reports of female disability often assume that anything less than 50% representation of women demonstrates inequity. The 50-50 rule drives or excuses much of the passion of women's advocacy. It is the semi-official reason to "wear the 'F' label with pride".[42] The rule is often the only analytical aspect of a disability claim. An example is an article titled "Gender imbalance in need of repair", which describes attempts to get women into male-dominated trades.[43] The article assumes that women avoid the construction, automotive and electro-technology workforce only because of stereotypes and opposition by a tribal culture, rejection and ridicule. Why else would women not want to be panel beaters? (A biological answer is reported below.) The effort is being made to benefit women by opening up work opportunities, though justification is sought in the universal good of economic efficiency. Pru

---

[41] "Sailor tells of her fear and distress after alleged spy episode in shower", *Sydney Morning Herald*, 1 May 2011, p. 3.

[42] *Sydney Morning Herald*, 7 Nov. 2011, p. 15.

[43] *Sydney Morning Herald*, 19-20 May 2012, Trades and Services Careers, p. 28.

Goward, the N.S.W. Minister for Women, explained that "[w]e need to work with industry to secure a competitive labour force in our state. . . industry can't afford to pick the best from only 50 per cent of the population". Strangely, the initiative did not come from employers or from government departments concerned with economics but from women's advocates.

The 50-50 rule also provided the rationale for a report critical of female underrepresentation in Australian theatrical companies. The press coverage of the report was limited to two data points: 21% of big productions had a female writer and 25% had a female director. The article did not quote any behavioural description of discrimination. The report stated that concerted efforts to "level the playing field" began 30 years earlier. But then it implied that not much levelling had been achieved, based only on the number of female writers and directors. On the same basis the sex ratio was described as inequitable and male directors were likened to arrogant monarchs. "It's embarrassing and protectionist and reeks of elitism", one interviewee was quoted as saying. The report suggested that one cause of female disability in this case was lack of superlatives for female achievement. Up-and-coming male directors and writers were described as "wunderkind", "hot" and "sexy" but there were no such terms for female talent.[44] The claim of disability was given some more solid backing by a subsequent letter to the editor from a management consultant involved in mentoring arts executives. Her practical (though uncosted) advice on how to boost female numbers was to "offer childcare, flexible work options, maternity leave and ongoing professional opportunities" as well as mentoring and leadership training.[45]

---

[44] "Australia Council finds women are bit players in theatre's 'feudal system'", *Sydney Morning Herald*, 24 April 2012, p. 1.

[45] "What's needed to keep women in the arts", *Sydney Morning Herald*, 26 April 2012, p. 10.

The arbitrariness and selective application of the 50-50 rule is apparent in some media reports. For example, the *Sydney Morning Herald* reported an improvement in the gender gap in starting salaries for graduates of Australian universities.[46] Overall, women still earn about 3% less than men in their first appointments, though there is considerable variation. Women do worst in earth sciences, earning 14.3% less. But in biological science they earn only 1.7% less than men. Curiously, the article does not report graduates' average grades. The claim of female disability would have been much stronger if the sexes had had the same quality of degrees across all disciplines. Compared to women, do men achieve better in earth sciences than they do in biology? If so, the market mechanism would be matching salary to qualification, at least to some degree. Further investigation might reveal more market influences. But these considerations are not part of the key statistics provided by the relevant government bureaucracy, the Equal Opportunity for Women in the Workplace Agency (EOWWA).[47] Neither are there relevant data on the government website responsible for documenting graduate careers.[48] The EOWWA does report that Australia has more women than men with degrees, both bachelor and postgraduate. But it is quality within discipline cohorts, not quantity overall, that is relevant to the equity question. The data provided are insufficient to conclude that there is any female disadvantage in starting salaries.

The rule looks shakier still considering that women's starting salaries often surpass those of men. This is the case in the physical sciences, the social sciences, veterinary science,

---

[46] "Gender salary gap improves as women graduates get ahead", *Sydney Morning Herald*, 6 Feb. 2012, p. 3.

[47] *http://www.eowa.gov.au/Information_Centres/Resource_Centre/Statistics/* GradStats_2011_12_PDF.pdf, *accessed 29 May 2012.*

[48] Graduate Careers Australia: *http://www.graduatecareers.com.au/*. In particular: *http://www.graduatecareers.com.au/research/exploreourresearch/ workandstudyoutcomes/*, accessed 29 May 2012.

agricultural science, social work, and pharmacy. Do women's grades surpass men's in these disciplines? Moreover, women outnumber men in many disciplines – in veterinary science the ratio is 80-20. This is a stunning violation of the 50-50 rule. Yet there were no letters to the editor protesting discrimination against men, no speculation about negative stereotypes of male vets, no calls for affirmative action scholarships to attract young men to university. In practice the criterion means the "at-least-50%-women-rule". The one exception was *Sydney Morning Herald* columnist Paul Sheehan's[49] call for post-feminist thinking. Sheehan noted that girls were outperforming boys at high school and that women were 60% of university undergraduates and almost the same percentage of postgraduates. He concluded that "society needs to address this growing imbalance". Sheehan was noting a trend already detected by the biosocial scientists Lionel Tiger in his 1999 book, *The Decline of Males*. Despite its irrationality the 50-50 rule has been in service for many years. In 1994 the then Chairman of the Australian Research Council stated that women were still under-represented at postgraduate level in some areas. "The fundamental difficulty is that there is a general lack of gender balance", he said.[50] The priority was not overcoming discrimination or lack of opportunity but building up the numbers of women. It would not have been much of an improvement in logic to argue that equalising the proportion of males and females would remove female disability; but it would have been principled.

The cavalier disregard of male disability is a remarkable feature of the women's movement. An example is the promotion of female representation with no sunset provisions. Consider the University of Western Australia's equity and diversity policy,

---

[49] Paul Sheehan, *Sydney Morning Herald*, 26 March 2012, p. 13.7

[50] Carruthers, F. (1994). "Women gaining ground by degrees." *The Australian*. Sydney, 18 April.

typical of the genre. It interprets the legislation as an open-ended mandate to employ women.

The Equal Opportunity for Women in the Workplace Act 1999 requires that the University formally adopts a policy and a programme for its implementation. One objective of this legislation is to improve the participation of women in all areas of employment.[51]

The goal of improving the participation of women "in all areas of employment" is revealing. There is no limiting clause, such as ". . . until unfairness is eliminated", despite the Act specifying its goals as the promotion of equal opportunity by removing barriers to women.[52] It seems inappropriate to increase women's participation where there is no evidence of disability. Genuine equal opportunity policy would advocate elimination of unfair discrimination without specifying any numerical targets. But if the 50-50 standard is to be adopted, consistency demands that men's participation should be encouraged when it falls below that level. The demand should become urgent when the disparity, either way, applies over a broad range, such as the 60-40 proportion of female-to-male graduates from Australian universities.

This lack of interest in men's disability conflicts with feminism's enabling ideology. The movement has sought legitimacy through its appeal to individualism and equality. Policies of equal opportunity and affirmative action are justified by appeals to fairness. No mandate has been secured from taxpayers to discriminate against men or perpetually favour women once equality of opportunity has been achieved.

---

[51] *http://www.hr.uwa.edu.au/policy/toc/appointment_and_employment/ equal_opportunity/eoaaps?childfx=on*, accessed 18 May 2012.

[52] *http://www.eowa.gov.au/About_EOWA/Overview_of_the_Act.asp*, accessed 30 May 2012.

The 50-50 rule is too useful to abandon. In the case of the *Herald* article on graduate pay, it was salvaged in two ways. First, there was no talk about male disability but much about the good news that some women were overcoming the gender pay gap. Secondly, the EOWWA stated that males had the advantage in 14 disciplines and women in only 6, and that the maximum male advantage in pay was greater than the maximum female advantage. The Agency's director concluded that the gender pay gap was still a problem. The same evidence allows us to conclude that males also suffer lower starting salaries in some disciplines or that perhaps there is not enough of a gap to worry about. Is it the season to prune the grievance bureaucracy? On the contrary, the Labor federal government is pressing ahead with anti-discrimination legislation that requires businesses to prove innocence when accused of bias.[53]

Female chauvinism. Categorical claims of women's superiority and disparagement of men are common in the media, despite the rejection of any hint that males might have their uses. An article that celebrated the rise of female executives of arts companies, stated: "Women are more collegiate as a rule, more focused on the objective, men have some other issues. They have been in roles longer and there is a great sense of entitlement."[54] Michelle Ryan, a British psychologist, suggested in an opinion article that women are better equipped to lead in times of crisis.[55] Such generalisations escape criticism or censorship. Even high-profile examples pass under the otherwise stern watchfulness of the PC police, such as this choice defamation from Germaine Greer: "Australian men generally avoid women; Englishmen actively torment and

---

[53] "Axe plan for sex bias laws: business", *Australian*, 6 Feb. 2012, p. 1.

[54] "Exhibiting talent, women run the shows", *Sydney Morning Herald*, 28-29 April 2012, p. 7.

[55] Michelle Ryan, "Woman on a ledge: females called upon to lead in times of crisis", *Sydney Morning Herald*, 8 March 2012, p. 11.

belittle them".[56] An example that combines chauvinism and a claim of female disability comes from a speech by U.S. president Barack Obama in May 2012. The speech was reported in the *New York Times* and was republished in the *Sydney Morning Herald*[57] without editorial comment.

Speaking to a graduating class at a women's college in New York City, Obama mixed reasonable values of equal opportunity with claims of female superiority. He regretted that only men signed the constitution in 1787 and criticised that document's failure to guarantee equality of sex and race. "[W]e can assume that there were founding mothers whispering smarter things in the ears of the founding fathers. [Applause.] I mean, that's almost certain." Obama decried the fact that women are 3 percent of Fortune 500 CEOs and occupy about 20 per cent of Congressional seats. He stated that the lack of women CEOs – in other words CEOs' maleness – was one cause of outdated workplace policies. Urging women to run for office, he concluded that "Congress would get a lot more done if you did."[58] The remark received laughter and applause, and neither the *New York Times* reporter or the *Herald* remarked Obama's sexism. Such rhetoric would have been condemned as bigoted if Obama had touted male superiority. Its acceptance by the leftist gatekeepers of public discourse raises doubts as to whether high principle is the only engine of feminism.

Invidious statements about men are sometimes combined with racial slurs, white males combining two favoured targets of cultural warriors of the left. The report on women's role in Australian theatre discussed earlier carried the quote: "[Artistic directors] say 'I only choose what's best'. So why is there a

---

[56] Germaine Greer, "Women's struggles go beyond one day", *Sydney Morning Herald*, 3-4 March 2012, p. 18.

[57] *SMH* 16 May 2012, p. 9, "Obama pitches for female votes".

[58] *http://www.ndtv.com/article/world/full-text-barack-obama-s-speech-at-barnard-college-210860*, accessed 16 May 2012.

predominance of white, middle-class men?"[59] In a *Sydney Morning Herald* opinion piece that made some interesting points, a female management consultant stated: "Most directors in boardrooms come from the same pool: pale, male and stale." The article made clear that staleness was due to paleness as well as maleness.[60]

Female success. These stories report the success of women in previously male-dominated occupations, and discuss how to further increase female representation. An example is a report on the fast food vendor McDonald's, 50% of whose senior executives are women, far above the 8% norm.[61] High ranking female police officers are given favourable mention[62] as are female executives and company board officers.[63]

Natural women. These are expressions of traditional female perspectives and values undisciplined by radical feminism, although they are sometimes written by women with feminist credentials. Such articles occasionally break through with a refreshing heterodoxy. We've already discussed Bettina Arndt, who quotes men and women bidding in the marriage market and writes about women's biological clock, being attractive and high-powered, and the fierce demand for quality men. In the *Sydney Morning Herald* Adele Horin reviewed research on the happiness brought by children, concluding that while there are

---

[59]   "Australia Council", *Sydney Morning Herald*, 24 April 2012, p. 1

[60]   "Diversity the answer for boardrooms", *Sydney Morning Herald*, 9 May 2012, p. 11.

[61]   "Taking McPride in gender policies", *The Australian*, 5-6 May 2012, Weekend Professional, p. 3.

[62]   *Sun-Herald*, 29 April 2012, pp. 16-17.

[63]   "Exhibiting talent, women run the shows", *Sydney Morning Herald*, 28-29 April 2012, p. 7.
       "Fewer obstacles on the way up", *Weekend Australian*, 10-11 March 2012, Weekend Professional, p. 2.

ups and downs, "[c]hildren are a gift that keeps giving".[64] Then there are women struck by the pangs of child hunger. "I will never be pregnant, never be protected by the father of my child, never be loved as the mother of his child, never love like you love, and never be loved as you're loved. I will never mean as much to anyone as you do. Imagine that, mums." This was written by a women in her 40s after realising she could not conceive.[65]

In the foregoing review I found little use of biological information. Science reporting on sex differences was thin and discussion of sex differences was rare. Apart from Bettina Arndt, most of the exceptions praised female superiority or criticised male shortcomings, such as Barack Obama's condescending speech. Neither did the themes reflect an even-handed concern for both sexes. I found only one report (by Sheehan) of male disability. The emphasis on female disability is reflected in the name of such government agencies as the Equal Opportunity for Women in the Workplace Agency. Cannot fairness cut both ways? Instead, as described above, the media frequently reflect hostility towards men. This hostility enjoys a privileged status, somehow evading censure.

Hostility is also directed at women who deviate from core radical feminist ideology, such as Bettina Arndt. In addition to critical reviews, gender studies students organised a demonstration against Arndt when she gave a talk at the Australian National University in 2011.[66] Arndt admits that her

---

[64] Adele Horin, "Children a gift that keeps giving", *Sydney Morning Herald*, News Review, 19-20 May 2012, p. 18.

[65] Bibi Lynch, "Mothers, stop moaning", *Sun-Herald*, Sunday Life, 13 May 2012, pp. 18-19. Originally: *http://www.guardian.co.uk/lifeandstyle/2012/mar/31/mothers-stop-moaning-about-motherhood*, accessed 29 May 2012.

[66] http://www.abc.net.au/unleashed/2758018.html, accessed 29 May 2012.

writing does not draw on that body of knowledge.[67] Academic lawyer Cathy Sherry described the intolerance shown towards feminists who oppose abortion. Although that is not her position, she had been subjected to vitriolic attack by left-feminists for expressing different views on women's issues.[68]

Gender studies in the universities

The near absence of behavioural biological content in media discussions of women and work raises questions about the content of gender studies courses at the nation's universities. Questions also arise from the double standard applied to male disability. What are they teaching our children, who go on to become journalists and commentators and teachers themselves? How true and wise are the theories and perspectives they provide? Could the situation be as bad as the 1980s and 1990s when the *Oxford Dictionary of Sociology's* entry for gender stated that socialisation, not biology, produces male and female behaviour?

To assess the place of biology in university gender studies programs I searched university websites. The Australian Women's and Gender Studies Association (AWGSA) lists related studies programs at Australian universities.[69] Among the 39 universities listed, links were provided to 23 departments and institutes at 21 universities. These 23 provided the focus of research. My search for biological content in these centres began with examination of the linked sites. This was a shallow sweep of all the links. Mentions of biology were to be followed up. There was no need. Of the 21 linked pages that contained information about course content, none mentioned hormones

---

[67] B. Arndt, personal communication, 6 May 2012.

[68] Cathy Sherry, "Feminism's clique does not help the cause", *Sydney Morning Herald*, 25 Jan. 2012, p. 15.

[69] http://awgsa.org.au/study, accessed 1 May 2012.

(endocrinology), animal models, genetics, ethology, sociobiology, behavioural ecology, evolution or evolutionary psychology. Such themes might have been named in further linked pages but they were not present on the initial pages or in the course lists examined. Ideological orientation varied from indeterminate to positions on the left. Sixteen of the centres expressed radical ideological leanings in course content, either through teaching about feminist theory, criticism of traditional society, or (only) female disadvantage. No courses expressed a conservative orientation, including anti-feminist criticism or pro-male advocacy. At least 8 centres taught gender in concert with other forms of "inequality" or "oppression", such as racism, colonialism and "heteronormativity".

Interestingly, gender studies is largely a female activity. Of the 12 institutions where faculty were listed, women are always the majority of academics. The larger institutions to which they belong have smaller proportions. The closest match was at the Australian National University, where the Department of Gender and Cultural Studies has 6 female faculty from a total of 11, while its host, the School of Culture, History & Language has 37 out of 107. That's 55% women in gender studies versus 35% in the enclosing faculty. At La Trobe University the corresponding figures are 78% and 53%; and at the University of Melbourne 75% and 50%. Lack of information about staff did not allow comparisons to be made at several universities. However, it is difficult not to read the sex ratios in gender studies as remarkable when there is a near absence of men. All the remaining schools for which data could be found – the gender studies programs at Flinders, Macquarie, Monash, Adelaide, N.S.W., and one at South Australia – taken together, have 102 female but only 7 male faculty. The disparity does not appear so extreme from a biological perspective. Naturally women are more interested in women's affairs than are men. The problems are analytical and ideological. Deviation from 50-50 is often taken as proof of discrimination or invidious stereotyping, used to justify and enforce reverse discrimination, the expenditure of public funds, and the reeducation of males. And it is done without reference to sex differences in interests or talents. If a skewed gender ratio among engineers or panel beaters is unacceptable, why not also among gender studies faculty? Why not among veterinary students or university students as a whole?

The absence of self-critical perspectives in gender studies centres indicates a robust level of solidarity or policing, also evident in the media. There appears to be few alternative theories or ideologies on the curriculum, certainly none that take biology seriously. It is what one would expect from a "tribal-moral" community as described by Jonathan Haidt[70] in the case of American social psychology.

I conclude that biology is generally overlooked in women's and gender studies in Australia. A probable contributing cause is that much of the field is monopolised by a radical ideological orientation which rejects inconvenient facts. To double check this finding I wrote to 20 heads of gender studies centres, those who could be identified. The 7 who replied confirmed that there is no behavioural biological content in their courses or research.

In defence of these gender studies centres it should be noted that many are not based in the social sciences. In those cases the absence of biology is a general characteristic of the humanities and not unique to gender studies. Neither does that situation reflect on the social sciences, except insofar as it has a duty to maintain standards of truth in other disciplines. However, 10 of the centres were either part of a faculty of social science or had an interdisciplinary makeup that included social science. Thus the foregoing survey of gender studies courses

---

[70] Haidt, J. (2011). "The bright future of post-partisan social psychology", Talk given at the annual meeting of the Society for Personality and Social Psychology, San Antonio, Texas, 27 Jan. *http://www.authorstream.com/Presentation/jhaidt-819710-haidt-postpartisan-social-psychology/*

provides further evidence that biology is omitted from Australian social science. The omission is doubly significant because no social phenomenon is more subject to biological analysis than gender.

Simone de Beauvoir's separation of sex and gender

Reading gender studies websites frequently turns up a famous aphorism coined by the French philosopher Simone de Beauvoir (1908-1986): "One is not born a women, one becomes one".[71] These words have become a core dogma of radical feminism, that culturally-based gender and biologically-based sex are distinct. De Beauvoir was especially interested in the question of self realisation, of the origin of womanly identity. She concluded that it was this gender identity that biology could not explain. Gender, the conscious experience of being a woman or a man and the cultural apparel and socially-imposed norms of femaleness and maleness, is independent of one's biological sex. In her view biology provides the body but not the mind of gender. A brief discussion of how de Beauvoir arrived at this view, and why it is false, offers clues as to how biosocial science might be reconnected to gender studies.

De Beauvoir's maxim is false because XX babies usually grow up to become self consciously women not due to coincidence or arbitrary social imposition but because biological sex causes them to acquire female consciousness and culture.

De Beauvoir's aphorism was formulated in her book, *The Second Sex*,[72] published in 1949, which examined the oppression of women. The book begins with an interesting and generally well-informed survey of the biological basis of sex.

---

[71] E.g. *http://sydney.edu.au/arts/gender_cultural_studies/undergrad/gender.shtml*, accessed 15 May 2012.

[72] Beauvoir, S. d. (1952/1949). *The second sex* [translated from the French]. New York, Alfred A. Knopf.

She knew about chromosomal determination. The book must be judged by the knowledge then available. For example, de Beauvoir claimed that the alleged passivity of the female is disproven by the equality of importance of the male and female gametes (p. 11). Although this an improbable view judged by present knowledge, de Beauvoir was opposing the equally improbable claim that the passivity of the female egg and the activity of the male sperm are inevitably reflected by the behaviour of women and men (pp. 13-14). Her discussion of how the endocrine system shapes the foetus into male and female was scientifically up to date, and is still in line with mainstream theory. Also up to date was de Beauvoir's discussion of the higher investment women make in reproduction, in line with sociobiological theory: "The production of sperms is not exhausting, nor is the actual production of eggs; it is the development of the fertilized egg inside an adult animal that constitutes for the female an engrossing task" (p. 24). This statement anticipated an important element of Robert Trivers' classic 1972 sociobiological paper[73] on parental investment. Like de Beauvoir, Trivers sees maternal investment as including care of the neonate. De Beauvoir implies the same in her view that women are irrevocably tied to the care of their children. Her formulation fell short of sociobiological theory mainly by omitting the connection between parental investment and reproductive fitness. The latter is not hinted at by de Beauvoir, for whom reproduction had vague psychological payoffs and many costs located in the conscious mind.

The lack of a usable theory of evolution is a signal weakness of de Beauvoir's biology. She had no concept of genetic interests or of how selection might have operated differently on the sexes to shape a different nature. Darwin had pointed the way to that with his concept of sexual selection, competition within a sex

---

[73]   Trivers, R. L. (1972). "Parental investment and sexual selection." *Sexual selection and the descent of man: 1871-1971*. B. Campbell (ed.). Chicago, Aldine: 136-179.

for sexual access to the other sex. In primates, competition occurs mainly among males, resulting in larger size, aggression, and appetite for risk. De Beauvoir might have taken satisfaction in knowing that in this regard the power balance is firmly with females because it is generally they who choose mates. Her evolutionary theory was limited to the notion that instincts are evolved to perpetuate the species (e.g. p. 36), a view out of favour among contemporary theorists. To be fair, the same error was made by most zoologists of the time. However, by the 1970s it was accepted that natural selection usually operates on individuals and small groups, rarely if ever on species as a whole. Knowing that might have led de Beauvoir to change her view that reproduction is a curse, a nuisance and an enslavement imposed by the species on women. Maintaining the myth of female victimhood would have required reconceptualising the slave masters to be overbearing men. Unfortunately for such a view, humans evolved in egalitarian societies where women usually had as much choice as men, more so in choosing mates. The realisation that women in their traditional roles, including tens of millennia of prehistory, have not been inferior to men and that their behaviour and intellectual prowess were equally adapted for survival and reproduction, shifts attention from the god of victimhood to the complexities of physiological and psychological adaptation. What de Beauvoir viewed as subordination, essentially from a chauvinistic male perspective, is in fact female behaviour playing a different game, where the winning condition is reproductive fitness in the form of thriving children and grandchildren. It was de Beauvoir's brand of feminism, her insistence on judging traditional women from the perspective of French intellectuals circa 1949, that was a greater slavery, which her writings have helped impose on future generations of feminists. Her dehumanisation of traditional women forms part of the Western intellectual elite's alienation from ordinary people, their history and continuity.

De Beauvoir's review of sex differences is not bad. It's what she failed to do with it that set her off on the path of gender unconnected with biology. For at the end of the chapter her matter-of-fact scientific exposition descended into metaphorical imprecision. For example, she declared that "society is not a species" as its customs cannot be deduced from biology. Individual members of society "are never abandoned to the dictates of their nature" because custom always takes over (p. 36). This separation of biology from gender is consistent with the near absence of social instinct in de Beauvoir's account of human nature. In her account there is male sexual aggression and female mothering and little else; nature produces mainly physiology, not sex-typical patterns of behaviour, preference and motivation. Culture alone supposedly governs gender, illustrated by examples of situations in which custom prevents masculine and feminine behaviours from asserting themselves. In situations where women get to choose their spouses, male initiative is powerless. And when society does not value the maternal bond it is not given recognition: "[T]his very bond . . . will be recognized or not according to the presumptions of the society concerned" (p. 36). This overlooks the general rule of female choice of mates and the universal importance of the mother-child bond. Some males devalue what mothers do for their babies but why adopt male values? Androcentrism hardly alters the social fact that in all societies it is normal for neonates to be cared for by their mothers. Female social power is demonstrated by the fact that no sustainable culture imposes separation of mother and baby.

De Beauvoir's emphasis of the male perspective and thus political-level power relations distracted her from the biological basis of social behaviour in general. How else could reproduction and child care for most of human existence, executed by an exquisite set of adaptations, be interpreted as nothing more than "enslavement of the female to the species" and the "limitations of her various powers" (pp. 36-7)? No wonder de Beauvoir is popular among the utopian-minded. Her doctrine that gender is wholly artificial and that it develops independently of biology allows speculative analysis and wishful thinking to soar unimpeded by stubborn biological facts. She was correct to conclude that biology is insufficient to fully explain gender relations. She was correct to include culture, economics and psychology as causes. Her error was to assume that biology affects the body and not consciousness or culture. The promise of her first chapter on biology is left unrealised, perhaps due to the rudimentary knowledge available in the 1940s or her overreliance on Hegel, Marx and Sartre. The biology of de Beauvoir's time could not explain gender identity, the conscious elixir around which *The Second Sex* revolves. We now know that gender identity is usually sex identity and is fixed by age three, when girls and boys begin rehearsing adult behaviour patterns that were adaptive for most of human existence. The cascade of events leading to gender identity involve environmental inputs but also innate biological processes and propensities at every stage.

Hormones and gender

The mainstream theory of mammalian sexual differentiation of behaviour received its first experimental confirmation just a decade after *The Second Sex* was published. Already in the 1930s it had been shown that the sexual behaviour of guinea pigs was affected by changing hormone balance. Then in 1959 a team of researchers led by William C. Young at the University of Kansas conducted another guinea pig experiment to test his hypothesis that prenatal hormones permanently organise the nervous system during critical periods in development.[74] The experiment showed that genetic female foetuses exposed to testosterone develop male sexual behaviour as adults. The

---

[74] Phoenix, C. H., R. W. Goy, et al. (1959). "Organizing action of prenatally administered testosterone propionate on the tissues mediating mating behavior in the female guinea pig." *Endocrinology* 65: 369-382.

resulting theory – that hormones shape the development of male and female nervous systems – has survived all tests in animals and humans and has become a cornerstone of behavioural endocrinology. The two effects are combined in the "organisational-activational theory", which has needed little amendment in the 50 years since Young and his students conducted their experiment. The theory allows for other factors, such as further hormonal organising effects during the critical period of adolescence and the direct action of X and Y genes.[75]

Interestingly, the pioneering breakthroughs in behavioural endocrinology were not informed by modern evolutionary theory. Instead, they used animal comparisons to guide the study of human physiology and brain structure. The approach resembled the classical ethologists who focused on the elucidation of a species' nature without bothering much about how that nature arose.

By the 1970s the theory was being tested on humans. John Money and Anke Ehrhardt's 1972 book, *Man and Woman, Boy and Girl: The Differentiation and Dimorphism of Gender Identity from Conception to Maturity*, reviewed evidence for the developmental effects of hormones. They reported that masculine and feminine physiology and behaviour were sensitive to pre-natal exposure to hormones. However, the data were incomplete at that stage, and Money and Ehrhardt concluded incorrectly that gender could be assigned to an individual of either genetic sex by hormonal intervention, even after the child was born. In particular, Money's animal experiments indicated that castration of neonate males and augmentation with female hormones reliably produced female gender, though lacking the physiology needed to conceive. He believed that humans acquired gender identity through social

---

[75] Arnold, A. P. (2009). "The organizational-activational hypothesis as the foundation for a unified theory of sexual differentiation of all mammalian tissues." *Hormones and Behavior* 55: 570-578.

learning. With body shapes to match, anyone could learn to adopt either gender identity. The first application of this hypothesis to humans failed. David Reimer, a normal boy whose penis has been removed by a botched circumcision was, on Money's advice, surgically and hormonally "reassigned" to female gender at the age of 18 months. Initially the reassignment seemed to work, though castration prevented the patient from conceiving children. The case was held up as an example of the fluidity of gender identity. However, Reimer behaved like a boy, even while having a female gender identity, and was teased by schoolmates. From his ninth year Reimer developed a male identity and in puberty began living as a male. He had reconstructive sex-change surgery and married. The case is evidence that gender identity is sensitive to prenatal and early childhood organisation of the nervous system and contributed to the decline in gender reassignment of normal XY males.[76] Evidence continues to mount in this direction. Gender identity is usually fixed by age three, consistent with innate influences. A 2004 study of 14 male (XY) babies reassigned as girls along the lines recommended by Money found that between ages 5 and 12 the procedure had proven unreliable in 8 children.[77] All 14 children showed moderate to marked masculine attitudes and interests. The authors of this study suggest that the high rate of reversion to genetic gender identity is due in part to direct action of X and Y genes on the nervous system.

By the 1990s the organisational-activational model of human sexual differentiation had accumulated strong empirical

---

[76] Diamond, M. and H. K. Sigmundson (1997). Sex reassignment at birth. Long-term review and clinical implications. *Archives of Pediatric and Adolescent Medicine*. 151(3):298-304; *http://www.hawaii.edu/PCSS/biblio/articles/1961to1999/1997-sex-reassignment.html*, accessed 30 May 2012.

[77] Reiner, W. G. and J. P. Gearhart (2004). "Discordant sexual identity in some genetic males with cloacal exstrophy assigned to female sex at birth." *New England Journal of Medicine* 350(4): 333-41. See review: *http://www.isna.org/node/564*, accessed 30 May 2012.

support. Many sex differences in brain organisation and associated behaviour had been identified.[78] It was known that women who were administered various hormones to treat at-risk pregnancies produced children who were feminised or masculinised relative to others of their own sex.[79] And the psychology of sex differences had matured, revealing similarity in general intelligence but major differences in some cognitive functions, such as average female advantage at verbal tasks, male advantage at spatial tasks.[80]

The left academic establishment continued to resist biological explanations of gender, despite converging evidence to the contrary. An instructive example is an exchange between Sandra Witelson, Professor of Psychiatry and Behavioural Neuroscience at McMaster University, Canada, and Richard Lewontin, Professor of biology at Harvard University.[81] Lewontin, an influential Marxist critic of all attempts to introduce biology to the social sciences, denied all biological causes of psychological sex differences. Despite advocating Darwinism against creationists, he repudiated all of Witelson's examples of hormonal effects on animal sex-typical behaviour and evidence of sex differences in humans. He found it relevant to claim that Jews were underrepresented in large corporations, and ended by suggesting that Witelson had not earned her professorship but was "simply a lucky fish who has wriggled

---

[78] Witelson, S. F. (1991). "Neural sexual mosaicism: Sexual differentiation of the human temporo-parietal region for functional asymmetry." *Psychoneuroendocrinology* 16: 131-153.

[79] Reinisch, J. M., M. Ziemba-Davis, et al. (1991). "Hormonal contributions to sexually dimorphic behavioral development in humans." *Psychoneuroendocrinology* 16: 213-278.

[80] Kimura, D. (1992). "Sex differences in the brain." *Scientific American* 266(September): 81-87.

[81] Witelson, S. F. (1985). "An exchange on 'gender' [with Richard Lewontin]." *The New York Review of Books*, *http://www.nybooks.com/articles/archives/1985/oct/24/an-exchange-on-gender/* [accessed 30 April 2012].

through a hole in the net meant to contain her." There is no room for doubt on this exchange. Lewontin represented ideology, Witelson the spirit of science. I recommend Witelson's 2011 talk at Moses Znaimer's Ideacity Conference on how sex differences in the brain and behaviour are hardwired.[82]

Australia had its own controversy over gender about the same time as Witelson confronted Lewontin. In 1985 Hiram Caton, professor of History and Politics at Griffith University, wrote a devastating criticism of a proposed course on women's studies at that institution. His objection was that the course contradicted and would keep students ignorant of many scientifically established biological influences on gender roles. He objected to a university teaching as true what was known to be false.[83] His argument was broad and rich with data. It was not based on sociobiological models but on behavioural endocrinology, physiology, psychology, and anthropology. The critique failed to prevent the proposal from being accepted. A colleague at the time and an advocate of the new course acknowledged that Caton's "sustained opposition" was the main obstacle encountered.[84]

The biological facts of sex differentiation falsify the notion that gender is independent of sex. They do not falsify all gender theory but constrain it. Biology determines whether an individual has male or female reproductive organs, and usually matches sexuality, brain structure and preferences. No change of customs, laws, beliefs, indoctrination, or practices have these effects. Sex identity involves learning, as de Beauvoir and Money supposed, but it can be difficult to persuade most

---

[82]　*http://www.ideacityonline.com/talks/sandra-witelson-on-neurological-differences-between-men-and-women/*, accessed 30 April 2012.

[83]　Southwood, E. (1986). "Hiram Caton vs. the radical feminists in fortress Griffith." Quadrant 30(220): 39-43.

[84]　Bullbeck, C. (1987). "Gender studies at Griffith University." Women's Studies International Forum 10(5): 537-541.

individuals that they belong to one gender when they feel or look or behave like the other. That was the experience of David Reimer and is that of many transgender individuals. The dichotomous identity of male or female is a biological given, although upbringing and culture dress that dichotomy in local colours. Like clothes, gender fits the preformed human body and mind, even though on occasion it is a bit of a squeeze.

Sex and work preferences

Beliefs about sex differences affect how we interpret data on proportions in the workplace. Female underrepresentation is usually interpreted as a problem to be rectified based on assumptions about stereotypes and male discrimination. Incorporating biology into the study of gender qualifies this assessment when the sex proportions are in line with known sex differences in preferences or abilities.

The entry of women in large numbers into the extra-household economy is a recent historical event. Their rise in the professions is even more recent. Clearly traditional gender roles have constricted female choice of careers. But what shapes those choices now that customary obstacles have receded? One would expect there to be much greater correspondence between individual preferences and gender proportions.

Support for this is provided by Kingsley Browne, a biosocial scientists at Wayne State University in Detroit, who uses behavioural biology to interpret work patterns.[85] He finds that in the United States the representation of the sexes corresponds largely to average sex differences in work preferences and abilities, which can be traced back to variation in hormones and ultimately to evolutionary history. Men show higher

---

[85] Browne, K. R. (2011). "Evolutionary psychology and sex differences in workplace patterns." *Evolutionary psychology in the business sciences*. G. Saad (ed.). New York, Springer: 71-94.

competitiveness, dominance-seeking, and risk-taking, while women show more nurturance. Men are oriented more towards objects, women towards persons. Differences in abilities can also play a role, for example men's greater upper body strength and some advantages in mathematics, and women's advantage at some spatial, computational, and verbal tasks. Browne notes than men are more willing to subordinate other activities, including family life, to achieve career success. They also run greater risks to gain advancement. Men also work longer hours and take on riskier and less pleasant work. To this can be added behavioural factors that advantage girls in education. Girls show lower rates of disciplinary problems and attention deficit disorder, both of which disadvantage boys educationally.

Browne makes the important point that a theory of broad female disadvantage cannot explain the highly variable sex ratios among work categories. As in Australia, women make up the great majority of graduates in veterinary science but a minority in engineering. Even within disciplines there are differences. In U.S. biology, women are 28% of graduates in entomology but 81% of those in nutritional science. In psychology, they are 55% of graduates in psychometrics and quantitative methods but 81% in child psychology. These variations are in line with sex-specific preferences. With respect to women's low representation in blue collar occupations, Browne agrees that "gendering" plays a part, in which some types of work are considered appropriate for only one sex. However, this explanation is "grossly incomplete", he argues, because it ignores coincidences of male preferences and abilities for these occupations. The analysis is completed with a review of the organising and activating effects of hormones and Darwin's theory of sexual selection.

I have given some space to Browne's thesis because it is a fine specimen of biosocial analysis, unifying the psychological, biomechanical and evolutionary levels of analysis. His theory might not be correct in every detail but has the huge edge in plausibility that it admits both social and biological causes, while competing theories, such as those found in gender studies, admit only social forces and insist on broad disadvantage, and only for women. In addition, biology theory explains much of the complex variability in sex ratios across work categories.

Gender relations and social technologies

Gender studies would not be made redundant if it were proven that female disability had largely been overcome, that from now on the battle of the sexes was a just war requiring no state intervention. The growing numbers of women, including in management roles, creates challenges for interpersonal relations and institutional design. In particular, women are rising in formal organisations through technical expertise and find themselves in positions that require managerial skills, where the job description includes exerting authority. Even with an all-male work force there were endemic problems related to the rise of specialist managers competing with generalists that parallel some of the issues faced by women and the glass ceiling. There is no need for women or men to accept being relegated just because the process that works against them is deemed fair. In sport as well as business someone headed towards defeat can legitimately deploy tactics that neutralise a competitor's winning tactic, so long as the methods used are ethical and legal.

An example is dominance. Browne correctly notes that men have greater ability to dominate than women, though there is overlap in the various components of the dominance repertoire. There is no avoiding the cut and thrust of dominance because the great majority of moves are part of everyday interactions. Dominance is usually legal and ethical, if not always polite. Most bullying is dominance behaviour but dominance is rarely bullying. An example is subtle stressors, for example ambiguous signalling of intent that causes a target to withdraw or concede. More subtle still, it is normal for actors to size up another individual, compute the likely outcome of a dominance contest with him or her, and avoid a losing strategy by withdrawing or preemptively submitting with appeasements. Consequently, dominance does not usually involve conflict. Alphas are generally relaxed and even friendly in established dominance relationships, but heated and unpleasant when their status is threatened.[86] This is not rocket science; much of it is intuitively understood and performed by implicit, subconscious cognition.

If it is fair for men to use their behavioural advantage in dominance to edge-out women (and sub-dominant men), it is also fair to neutralise that advantage. Three types of countermeasures have been attempted. Women have formed coalitions to overcome individual male dominance. This makes sense because men are also adept at forming empowering coalitions, perhaps more so than women. A second tactic has been for women to beef up their dominance repertoire. This can be successful to a point. Human cognition has some ability to override implicit motivation. On the receiving end, knowing that a certain stimulus is likely to induce subordinate motivation can allow the conscious mind to block otherwise automatic responses. Appropriate responses can be rehearsed. The power of the conscious mind to override instinctive responses makes many sociobiological mechanisms negotiable. Sandra Witelson recommends that women make themselves aware of hard-wired tendencies that can stiffen the glass ceiling. She picks out aversion to risk as one female characteristic that helps reduce the number of women high-flyers. One obstacle to simulating dominance behaviours is that some, such as low voice pitch, are generated physiologically. The tactic they embody is the result of evolution, not human cognition.

---

[86]   Salter, F. K. (2008/1995). Emotions in command: Biology, bureaucracy, and cultural evolution. New York, Transaction.

With regard to signal quality, Margaret Thatcher famously sought to sound more impressive by training her speaking voice to a lower timbre. In effect, she saw politics as a drama in which she was a performer. The late Erving Goffman, the urban anthropologist, would have seen Thatcher's public persona as well crafted self-presentation. Thatcher showed that instinct is negotiable to a point. Managerial dramaturgy can be carried off if the poses become automatic and sustainable, which requires consistency with the actor's personality. However, it can be difficult to emulate the subtleties of spontaneous dominance tactics. For example, men who judge themselves dominant to another male subconsciously lower their voice pitch when addressing him, but raise their pitch when they consider themselves less dominant.[87]

The third tactic is to deploy social technologies. These are devices, including rules, routines, architecture and ideologies, that regulate behaviour. The theory of social technology was developed by ethologists and political theorists and overlaps the sociological concept of "social control". But unlike sociological approaches, social technology theory does not deny the existence of hard-wired behaviour. Social technologies manipulate instincts as well as learned behaviours. Among the earliest of these technologies were architectural structures that directed attention to a central point, obviating the attention-getting component of dominance. Examples include throne rooms, amphitheatres and temples. In these settings anyone, no matter how unprepossessing, who occupies the focal point, can attract attention more readily than others. The routine, low-key attraction of attention is a necessary component of established dominance hierarchies. It is a feature of the formal organisation. The latter favours women because it allows

---

[87] Puts, D. A., S. J. C. Gaulin, et al. (2006). "Dominance and the evolution of sexual dimorphism in human voice pitch." Evolution and Human Behavior 27(4): 283-296.

anyone of technical competence to acquire the powerful means of dominance that go with line office.

Formal organisation is an assemblage of social technologies that negates the most powerful dominance behaviours. It has been argued that women are disadvantaged in bureaucracies because feminine attributes are subordinate ones.[88] On the contrary, femininity is most disadvantageous where men are unrestrained. Bureaucracy offers special advantages to women. Feminine interpersonal behaviour is most advantaged in environments disciplined by a degree of separation between office and person. Codes of courtesy are another social technology that inhibit dominance, because they target aggressive tactics.

Managers and aspiring managers should know how dominance interacts with organisational structure and how to mobilise the soft power of courtesy to regulate feral tactics. They should know the difference between the aggressive behaviours used to win dominance, which can disrupt work groups, and the more benign types shown by dominants once in power, which promote team effort. They should know the tell-tale signs of dominance when it is deployed dramaturgically or as felt emotion. They should know how emotions are distributed down a hierarchy in times of peace and conflict. They need to know the difference between legitimate and illegitimate tactics and how to move the dividing line. And they should understand how the organisational environment systematically changes the rules of dominance, turning otherwise competitive displays into faux pas that undermine authority.

Courtesy applied to social tactics has teeth. It tends to neutralise overt dominance tactics by incurring heavy social costs. In courteous social environments, ambitious young males

---

[88]   Ferguson, K. E. (1984). The feminist case against bureaucracy. Philadelphia, Temple University Press.

who use a booming voice and interruption to suppress others' input can be legitimately brought to heel, *in their tactics*, by ostracism and intervention by management. The courtesy code should also be imposed on high ranking line managers, male or female, who exploit their power to establish heavy-handed dominance. This corruption of office harms not only the manager's social standing but the cohesion and morale of work groups. It is the antithesis of effective leadership. Like other markets, the intersection of gender and work will always produce pockets of rigidity, monopoly, and enthusiastic buying and selling. Regulatory intervention in the form of equity measures should remain an option. But when the playing field is reasonably level, which it has become, women should join men in fending for themselves. Why should not everyone benefit from his natural endowments?

Remedies

What can be done to prevent departments of gender studies from teaching as true what is known to be false, such as that there are no hardwired behavioural sex differences? The situation is unacceptable, though perhaps not as grim as the late David Stove suggested in his *Quadrant* article of May, 1986, in which he argued that feminism of the Marxist variety had contributed to turning faculties of arts at Western universities into disaster areas akin to badly-leaking nuclear reactors.[89] While this is surely an exaggeration, nothing violates universities' ancient values more than teaching what is known to be false. As a result real damage is being done to the knowledge of generations of students and to the nation's political culture.

Departmental or institutional self-correction of anti-biological bias would be the best remedy. That would be most likely to

---

[89] *http://web.maths.unsw.edu.au/~jim/arts.html*, accessed 30 May 2012.

occur in an interdisciplinary milieu rich in collaboration between gender analysts and behavioural biologists. But that would entail a breach of disciplinary boundaries, and the social sciences have protected their turf against the harder disciplines for at least two generations and are unlikely to change overnight. By themselves, universities are probably unable to correct the situation because gender studies' parent tribal-moral community is hegemonic within the university sector. At present gender studies, partly sheltered within the social sciences, is anything but compromised by its anti-biological dogma. It will continue to be fed by taxpayer funds and supported by elements of the mainstream media, some government bureaucracies, and the intellectual left.

Some types of political intervention would be legitimate, for example legislation that paralleled laws mandating equity programs or that established procedures to deal with corruption. Intervention aimed at restoring truth in teaching could not reasonably be construed as violating the university's mission or its intellectual autonomy if the standard of truth came from within. New laws that equalise the status of men and women would be ethical and would help sever any unseemly feedback that might exist between ideological solidarity and appointments. For example, the 50-50 rule should apply when either sex is in the minority or be formally rescinded as an element of equity programs. There is also the question of effectiveness. Which measures would correct the situation with least collateral damage? Sunset clauses might limit harm but do not guide content. Is there, in principle, a legislative magic bullet? To give a negative example, the problem is not of a kind to be solved by sacking university boards, as Hiram Caton recommended in 1985. Nor would it be wise to excise (or reassign) gender studies programs as a structural category. Even if such a measure were politically feasible, gender is too important a subject to sacrifice, as is the expertise accumulated by scholars in the field. The goal should be one of augmentation, not amputation. But how? How to drag gender studies and the social sciences in general into the larger world of science?

One model is the requirement that all technical students, such as scientists and engineers, undertake courses in the humanities and social sciences. The principle could be applied to gender studies and the social sciences. One broad measure could be to require departments of social science, including centres of gender studies, to interact with behavioural biologists. For example, courses dealing with a phenomenon could be required to include instruction in relevant biological knowledge, taught by experts from the relevant discipline, and overseen by a board of interdisciplinary studies. Another measure would be to direct funding agencies under government control to favour cross-disciplinary research proposals that integrate the social and life sciences.

The pragmatic question is whether the conservative political parties will take the lead in pushing through reform. That depends on whether they see university departments of gender studies or social science as a political nuisance. Such a perception is more probable the longer those disciplines remain wedded to the left side of politics.

Government intervention would be regrettable. State meddling in universities is inherently clumsy and dangerous to academic freedom. However, the same can be said of entrenched ideological monopolies.

Australia and the National Question Part I: The Media

For the intellectual left that came to power in the 1960s and 1970s, no front of the culture wars is more important than the national question – what constitutes a nation, the benefits and costs of nationhood, the connections between national identity and interests, ethnic and racial differences, and the proper relations between nation, state, immigration, domestic ethnic groups and other countries. Four of the five taboos in the social sciences identified by Jonathan Haidt are related directly or indirectly to these issues: race differences; blaming the victim; stereotype accuracy; and nativism.[90]

Leftist values are not intrinsically anti-national. In the 19th and first half of the 20th centuries Western elites often combined affection for their peoples with liberalism, including support for expanded civil rights. The Christian drive to end slavery in the late 18th century was not associated with unpatriotic sentiment. Labour movements have often supported protectionism and restrictive immigration in alliance with conservatives. However, as Eric Kaufmann has documented, the internationalist strand in socialist thought rose to prominence during the course of the

---

[90]   Haidt, J. (2011). "The bright future of post-partisan social psychology", Talk given at the annual meeting of the Society for Personality and Social Psychology, San Antonio, Texas, 27 Jan. *http://www.authorstream.com/Presentation/jhaidt-819710-haidt-postpartisan-social-psychology/*

20th century.[91] From before the Bolshevik coup of 1917 cosmopolitans, as Kaufmann terms them, have fought against beliefs that would bolster Western identity and confidence.

One such activist was Columbia University anthropology professor Franz Boas who helped supplant the nascent biosocial sciences in the United States with the cosmopolitan New Social Sciences. Boas's opposition to biosocial science is valorised as "scientific anti-racism" which he pioneered in a famous publication of 1912.[92] The research purported to demonstrate that races rapidly converge on a common type when living in the same country. His goal was to assuage Anglo-American concerns that mass immigration would alter national identity. Boas was so strongly motivated in this direction that he opposed all biological theories of human nature. To that end he abandoned liberal and academic standards. Despite evincing the values of the 1848 liberal revolutionaries, he remained a stalwart of the Soviet Union through the Ukrainian genocide of 1931-2. On the scientific side, he doggedly supported official Soviet Lamarckianism, the theory that characteristics acquired by individuals during their lifetimes are passed on genetically to children. Boas remained a Lamarckian long after the theory was discredited in scientific circles. He approved Margaret Mead's deeply flawed doctoral thesis on Samoan teenage sexuality that attributed white puberty blues to pathologies of Western civilisation. His 1912 research, a keystone document in the effort to radicalise American social science, was recently shown to be fallacious, not in the data collected by junior colleagues but in the statistical analysis conducted by Boas, a master statistician.[93] Subsequent attacks on biosocial conceptions of ethnicity and nationhood have frequently been tempted to trade truth for ideology.

---

[91] Kaufmann, E. (2004). *The rise and fall of Anglo-America*. Cambridge, MA, Harvard University Press.

[92] Boas, F. (1912). "Changes in bodily form of descendants of immigrants." *American Anthropologist* 14(3): 530-562.

I am not suggesting that the pioneer leftist social scientists were Soviet agents. But they were sympathetic. For example John Dewey, held by Kaufmann to have cofounded the New Social Sciences with Boas, was not a Stalinist. Neither was he a revolutionary. But he did move in far-leftist circles and in 1937 chaired the Commission of Inquiry into the Charges Made against Leon Trotsky in the Moscow Trials, organised by a Trotskyist front organisation that included Boas. The Commission concluded that Trotsky had been loyal to the revolution.

A century after Boas the flaws in Marxist economics are understood but communist doctrine regarding the national question is triumphant. This is manifested intellectually in a near absence of biology in media and academic discussions. Politically it is evident in the intolerant utopianism of multiculturalism, revolutionary levels of immigration, and censorship of free speech on the subject.

The loss of this front of the culture wars had unhinged the West's political leadership's capacity to comprehend ethnic affairs in a growingly diverse and mobile world. The same political elite that was surprised when the Soviet Union broke up into its constituent nations – because they did not perceive it to be an empire consisting of captive nations praying for release – is also managing the progressive swamping of Western nations by mass immigration. The policy is fascinating from the evolutionary perspective because it is drastically reducing Western populations' collective fitness. Not everything about the process is new. Displacement of populations through colonisation has been happening since time immemorial, usually on a much smaller scale. What distinguishes the present situation throughout much of the West is that it was not

---

[93] Sparks, C. S. and R. L. Jantz (2002). "A re-assessment of human cranial plasticity: Boas revisited." *Proceedings of the National Academy of Science www.pnas.org* 99(23): 14636-14639.

initiated by armed invasion. Instead, colonisation is occurring at the invitation of Western elites, often contrary to public opinion. The process is epochal whether viewed through zoological, national, or democratic eyes.

Media coverage

The national question figures large in the Australian media. I collected 215 articles and programs on national themes, mainly from the *Sydney Morning Herald* (henceforth the *Herald*) but also from the *Australian* and selected television and radio programs, from September 2011 until August 2012. The *Herald* is part of the Fairfax media group, which occupies a position analogous to the *New York Times* in America, from which it often reprints articles. The *Australian* is the flagship of Rupert Murdoch's media empire in Australia, which owns most of the country's print media. The newspaper reflects the Murdoch formula of a campaigning approach to journalism with a neoconservative flavour.

The collected media reports discussed Aborigines, refugees, white racism, the benefits of multiculturalism and diversity, criticism of white Australia, national identity (including Anzac Day), foreign investment, international relations, and overseas ethnic conflict.

As expected, there were almost no references to biological factors. A rare exception was a *Herald* report of a scientific study concerning the evolution of racial differences (SMH 16.8.2012, p. 18). Though this was not mentioned in the article, this area of research is relevant to studies of ethnic conflict and diversity because it bears on the significant genetic differences between ethnic groups and races.[94] Genetic differences between groups entails genetic similarity within them, which typically

---

[94]   Cavalli-Sforza, L. L., P. Menozzi, et al. (1994). *The history and geography of human genes*. Princeton, New Jersey, Princeton University Press.

resembles that found among cousins and can be as high as that found among half siblings or grandparent and grandchild. This makes ethnic groups vast pools of kinship for their members, and helps explain the passions that frequently characterise ethnic affairs.[95]

Another exception to the dearth of biology concerned medical differences between Australians of Aboriginal and European descent. In a radio interview conducted by Alan Jones in July 2012, Dr. Alan Barclay of the Australian Diabetes Council stated that Caucasians have a lower prevalence of diabetes than indigenous Australians.[96] He explained that the risk of Type II diabetes rises after aged 45 for Whites but after age 35 for Aborigines, due to different evolutionary backgrounds. Caucasians have had agriculture for many thousands of years and become genetically adapted to more sugar in their diet. Neither man remarked that this information contradicts a mantra of multicultural ideology, that racial differences are biologically insignificant, that they are skin deep because populations have not been separated long enough for evolution to occur. Perhaps medical professionals should explain to social scientists that race differences go down at least to the pancreas and that substantial divergent evolutionary change has occurred in the last 10,000 years.[97]

The most impressive discussion of biosocial themes was on the SBS television program *Insight* on 20 April 2012. SBS provides content in languages other than English and on themes of interest to non-Anglo audiences. Dr. Fiona Barlow, a social

[95]   Harpending, H. (2002). "Kinship and population subdivision." *Population and Environment* 24(2): 141—147.
       Salter, F. K. (2007/2003). *On genetic interests. Family, ethnicity, and humanity in an age of mass migration.* New York, Transaction.

[96]   Alan Jones Show, Radio 2GB, 9 July 2012.

[97]   Cochran, G. and H. Harpending (2009). *The 10,000 year explosion: How civilization accelerated human evolution.* New York, Basic Books.

psychologist in the School of Psychology, University of Queensland, explained that racism has an innate basis. Some individuals are more predisposed to develop racist attitudes than others. Humans have a cognitive bias to remember harmful but not pleasant behaviour from members of other ethnic groups, and to attribute it to that group. That is a "normal, natural" thing to do.[98] The same program showed a video clip of an evolutionary psychologist, Prof. Doug Kenrick of Arizona State University, explaining how ethnocentrism evolved. Humans are quick to suspect the motives of strangers from other ethnic groups but are also adept at calculating the risks and rewards to be gained from interaction. The evolutionary analysis of ethnic affairs does not indicate automatic racism. These contributions were valuable but did not fully develop the theme of the normality of ethnocentrism. Not only racism but prosocial values of ethnic and national community have an innate basis. And if minority ethnic consciousness is normal, so is the majority equivalent.

The general absence of biosocial perspectives was evident in the media's lack of interest in signs of ethnic hierarchy. Pecking orders interest zoologists. They are ubiquitous in vertebrate species. Ethnic hierarchy is relevant to the national question because a fundamental legitimation for government is that it protects the people from conquest. In the Western tradition that is the first duty of sovereigns. A king might have exploited his subjects but in defence of the realm ruler and ruled shared an interest in resisting external domination. In anthropological theories of the state, hunter-gatherers gave up their egalitarian social structure in the interests of group defence. Still today, in liberal doctrine, liberty from external subjugation takes precedence over citizens' individual civil liberties within the

---

[98] *Insight*, 20 April 2012, first interview;
http://www.sbs.com.au/insight/episode/watchonline/459/I-m-Not-Racist-But...,
accessed 23 April 2012, at about 12 mins.

state.[99] (Libertarians are right to see war as a threat to their values.) This made good evolutionary sense because conquered populations lose resources including territory and, ultimately, reproductive fitness.

Yet the Australian elite media show little interest in ethnic hierarchy, beyond alleging white racism. If provoked into commenting on the subject, many would reply that multi-culturalism has done away with the only ethnic hierarchy Australia has known, which saw Anglo-Celtic Australia firmly on top and Aborigines and non-English-speaking immigrants firmly underneath. This thesis makes sense for most of Australian history since 1788 but not in recent decades. Anglo-Celtic Australians are being rapidly displaced by mass Third World immigration they were never asked to approve, are excluded from multicultural forums, and are the prime targets of political correctness, including a growingly coercive legal apparatus.

Anglo-Celtic Australia's subordinate status is also indicated by the pattern of media reporting and commentary on ethnic affairs. An element of that pattern is the emphasis on white racism. Journalists are alert for discrimination when practised by Anglo Australians but are somnolent in the case of minorities. This is odd from the biosocial perspective because ethnocentrism is a species characteristic, a universal potentiality. Ethnic networking and other forms of solidarity are usually most intense in minorities.[100]

Following in chronological order are examples of criticisms of Anglo and white Australians.

[99] Skinner, Q. (1998). *Liberty before liberalism*. Cambridge, Cambridge University Press.

[100] Salter, F. K. (2002). *Risky transactions: Trust, kinship, and ethnicity*. New York, Berghahn Books.

Sports journalist Patrick Smith criticised Tiger Woods' former caddy for calling Woods a "black arsehole" despite the caddy apologising. Smith was so outraged that he rounded on the sport itself: "As for men's golf, well, it is seen for what it always has been. A white sport played and administered protectively by white men." (*The Australian*, 9 Nov. 2011[101]).

Herald columnist Ruth Ritchie (26-27 Nov. 2011) reviewed a television show featuring a pair of Muslim comedians who "share, with rapier wit, how it feels to be hated by white people. . . . And their observations about idiotic WASP male conversation is as keenly observed as any woman's."[102]

After describing an English commentator as "a fraud and a mountebank", columnist Angela Shanahan wrote: "It is an English thing, the Oxbridge talent for shock, fury and fulmination all delivered in the closed-mouthed plummy accent." (*Herald*, 24-25 Dec. 2011[103])

Peter Gebhardt, a retired County Court Judge, wrote: "Australia Day is, of course, an artificial fabrication designed by governments, . . . and smug Anglo-Saxons to ensure that we forget real history. That Anglo-Saxon smugness is a resilient child of hypocrisy and racism. . . . . . . It is only the resilience and the strength, the honesty and the earth-strength of the Aboriginal people that has enabled them to survive . . .every conceivable peril placed in their paths by the whites who rely on a specious superiority." (*Herald,* 26 Jan. 2012, online[104]).

---

[101] Patrick Smith, "White man's game could show Woods some respect", *The Australian*, 9 Nov. 2011, Sport, p. 33.

[102] Ruth Ritchie, "Crossing the racial divide", *SMH*, 26-27 Nov. 2011, Spectrum, p. 18.

[103] Angela Shanahan, "An intellectual to learn from and a fraud to recoil from", *SMH*, 24-25 Dec. 2011, p. 18.

[104] Peter Gebhardt, "Nation's day a chance to shine a light into the darkness", *SMH*, 26 Jan. 2012, online.

SBS TV newsreader Mary Kostakidis wrote: "Commercial television is still the province of middle-aged white male fantasy – non-white faces and older women are sent to Coventry." (*Herald,* 3-4 March 2012[105])

Germaine Greer's combination of sexism and anti-Anglo chauvinism is published without editorial protest: "Australian men generally avoid women; Englishmen actively torment and belittle them" (*Herald,* 3-4 March 2012[106]).

On SBS television Toby Ralph, a marketing strategist, criticised the negative stereotyping of an Indian actor in a banned television advertisement, calling it racist. He then characterised an actress in the same advertisement as "this pert little Caucasian blonde who is like a sexualised Hitler youth" (*Insight,* SBS, 20 March 2012[107]).

In May 2012 Helen Szoke, Australian Race Discrimination Commissioner, stated that Anglo Australians have a special problem with racism not found in other ethnic groups. "People who are part of the majority grouping, the white Anglo-Saxon grouping" deny that their discrimination is racist. Szoke painted a picture of an insensitive Anglo Australia which is not giving enough opportunities to Aborigines or immigrants of non-English speaking background. "[T]he white Australia policy is still part of the 'muscle memory' of the more homogenised white Australia." (p. 21). The evidence for this strong claim was weak.[108] Typical for anti-discrimination advocacy from its

---

[105] Mary Kostakidis, "A diversified media can tell humanity's myriad stories", *SMH,* 3-4 March 2012, New Review, p. 16).

[106] Germaine Greer, "Women's struggles go beyond one day", *SMH,* 3-4 March 2012, p. 18.

[107] *Insight,* SBS Television, 20 March 2012. Transcript at: *http://www.sbs.com.au/insight/episode/transcript/459/I-m-Not-Racist-But*

[108] The evidence of Anglo racism consisted of a fall in the proportion of Aborigines in government employment, too many whites in advertising and free-to-air television, and a fall is social cohesion.

earliest days, these disparaging remarks were not balanced by a discussion of non-Anglo networking or anti-social behaviour or, on the other side of the ledger, success and overrepresentation in important areas such as higher education, selective schools, the professions, and areas of business.[109] No mention was made of group interests, for example the cost to the Anglo community of affirmative action for minorities or infrastructure for immigrants. Racism is seen only in Anglos and whites. It gets worse. Szoke described how her own family has been adversely affected by Australian discrimination. "Here [Australia], our psyche has been scarred . . . We'll have to wait and see what happens" (p.22) (*Law Society Journal*, May 2012[110]). The components of this story sit uncomfortably together – the categorical criticisms of Anglo Australians, the failure to consider ethnic interests, and the Commissioner's personal ambivalence towards the same ethnic group that she officially condemns. The combination looks dangerous when she calls for the criminalisation of racial vilification (*Herald*, 30 Aug. 2012[111]). This is not an aberration. The problem is systemic and fits the left-minority coalition's broader effort to discourage white dissent and only white dissent.

On Anzac Day in late April, which commemorates soldiers' sacrifice for the nation, Eva Cox of the University of Technology, Sydney, doubted that Anzac Day was for all Australians because it is "very Anzac Anglo" (*Sun-Herald*, 29 April 2012, p. 86). In his Anzac comment, historian Craig Stocking sought to soften the clash between national identity

---

[109] Wilkinson, P. (2007). The Howard legacy: Displacement of traditional Australia from the professional and managerial classes. Essendon, Australia, Independent Australian Publishers.

[110] Anne Susskind, [Interviews Helen Szoke], *Law Society Journal*, May 2012, pp. 20-22.

[111] Dan Harrison, "Calls for federal law to criminalise racial abuse", *SMH*, 30 Aug. 2012, p. 5. *http://www.smh.com.au/national/calls-for-federal-law-to-criminalise-racial-abuse-20120829-2512p.html*

and the multicultural population by exploding misconceptions about Australian soldiers. True, the Anzac legendary hero is "always, always white", but thankfully Australia's behaviour on the battlefield has had nothing to do with its soldiers being Australian, with their national character or "ethnic inheritance" (*The Australian*, 25 April 2012). As Peter Coleman succinctly puts it, "Leftist writers, who do not like Australia or Australians, have assembled a portfolio of charges to debunk 'the Anzac myth'."[112] There is also the minority ethnocentric motive, usually expressed in leftist tropes. Aboriginal activist Noel Pearson feels distant from Anzac Day because it is "too white", despite him also maintaining that race is an irrelevant category. The ritual is nauseating because it distracts whites from the more worthy memory of his own people's suffering.[113] Australia's wars have been fought overwhelmingly by Anglo and other white Australians. So recent was the start of mass non-European immigration –since the 1970s – that the minority segment of the population does not yet figure in the core national identity as accumulated in images and memories of war heroes, veterans, war diaries and correspondence, casualty lists, war memorials, and war leaders. The same can be said of our explorers, pioneers, leaders, writers, scientists, and of the imprint of culture, law, and political institutions.

The change has been so rapid that veterans can notice. An example was publicised during Anzac Day in 2011 when Jim Wallace, head of the Australian Christian Lobby, commented in an online message that Australians should "remember the Australia [veterans] fought for – it wasn't gay marriage and Islamic" (*The Australian*, 26 April 2011[114]). He sent the message

---

[112]   Coleman, P. (2012). "Australian notes". *Spectator Australia*. London, The Spectator Ltd., p. vi.

[113]   Noel Pearson, 2011, *Up from the mission: Selected writings*, Collingwood, Victoria: Schwartz Media, p. 337.

[114]   "Christian lobbyist sorry for gays, Islam tweet", *The Australian*, 26 April 2011.

– which is true – after watching the Anzac Day march on television with his 96 year-old father, a veteran of Tobruk and Milne Bay. The message provoked a storm of protest. Predictably he was called racist, despite the religious theme. The message is also true when applied to ethnicity and race. Australian did not fight for diversity or to see their descendants become an ethnic minority. Among the reasons soldiers fought, the most common ideal was probably the aspiration for national freedom. That reality, combined with the majoroty Anglo makeup of the Anzacs, makes Australia's past a foreign country for those alienated from the historical nation.

A *Herald* opinion piece complained that Australian board rooms were too white and too male and that both deficiencies contributed to their staleness (9 May 2012).[115]

Herald education editor Andrew Stevenson claimed in a front page article that private schools are insufficiently diverse. The headline contained a racial slur which indicated that insufficiently diverse meant too white: "The white bread playground: top private schools shun ethnic diversity" (12 June 2012).

The ABC2 television program *Dumb, Drunk and Racist*, June to July 2012, presented harsh images of Anglo Australians.[116] Mainly white Australians were shown displaying ethnic hostility and abusing alcohol. The anchor, Joe Hildebrand, a journalist for the Murdoch-owned Daily Telegraph, invited four Indians to fly to Australia and pass judgement on Australian race relations. Indians were chosen because that country has an especially negative view of Australian racism. The show focused on displays of racial abusiveness in interactions claimed by Hildebrand to be purely spontaneous: "The truth is virtually

---

[115] "Diversity the answer for boardrooms", *Sydney Morning Herald*, 9 May 2012, p. 11.

[116] *http://www.abc.net.au/tv/dumbdrunkracist/*, accessed 30 Aug. 2012.

every confrontation, every bit of violence or abuse, was caused by people we just happened to accidentally stumble across – or rather who just came across us."[117] This seems a hazardous way of organising a costly documentary. But we need go no further than Hildebrand's own views to detect bias. In the second episode of the series, his response to the view that immigrants should adopt Australian customs was: "[N]ot sure what Australian customs there are, maybe drinking, gambling, wearing stubbies."

Sports reporter Simon Barnes's London *Times* article on Wimbledon was reprinted in the *Weekend Australian*: "I can never watch Serena Williams without being overwhelmed by a race-guilt for all the terrible things that white people have done to non-white people over the centuries" (7-8 July 2012[118]).

A candidate for council elections was reported in the *Herald* as opposing Sharia law and praising Australian in contrast to Muslim culture. The reporter, Nicole Hasham, implied that the candidate was a "racial supremacist" (21 Aug. 2012[119]).

In the context of criticising the Federal Parliament for insufficient ethnic diversity, columnist George Megalogenis implied that the institution is too white and that whiteness reduces openness: "It has become more monochrome at the very moment we need to pursue more openness – in markets and in immigration." (*Weekend Australian*, 21-22 July 2012[120])

The Foreign Minister Bob Carr criticised the Opposition leader, Tony Abbott's, statement that Australia belongs to the

---

[117] http://www.thepunch.com.au/articles/so-it-turns-out-plenty-of-us-are-dumb-drunk-and-racist/, accessed 30 Aug. 2012.

[118] *The Weekend Australian*, 7-8 July 2012, Sport, p. 39.

[119] Nicole Hasham, "Politics of prejudice as cultural cowboys court xenophobic vote", *SMH*, 21 Aug. 2012, p. 3.

[120] George Megalogenis, "Reform blues stem from parliament's monochrome demography", *Weekend Australian*, 21-22 July 2012, Inquirer, p. 22.

Anglosphere. He linked the statement to the anti-Asian views of One Nation founder Pauline Hanson in the 1990s. "With our heritage of White Australia and membership of the British Empire . . . it's too risky for us even to glance in the direction of talk of an Anglosphere. It revives all those unfortunate recollections and associations." (*Weekend Australian*, 28-29 July 2012[121]).

In the context of criticising Christian missionaries, Phillip Adams's accusations became racial: "The spiritual destruction of aboriginal religions throughout the world by white invaders was finally far worse . . ." (*Weekend Australian*, 4-5 Aug. 2012[122]).

It seems that the elite Australian media do not always report events as objective observers but as participants, and that when they participate in ethnic issues they sometimes adopt a hostile attitude towards Anglo and white Australia but not towards minorities.

The gentle reception of anti-Anglo defamation

Sometimes what is *not* stated in the media points to bias. The media routinely pass over chauvinism and racism when directed at Anglo Australians. An example is *Herald* journalist Jane Cadzow's criticism of Aboriginal activist Noel Pearson's verbal abuse of government officials and reporters as "f**king white c***s". She did not dwell on the remark's racist content (*Herald*, 25 Aug. 2012[123]). The same was true of journalist Tony Koch's original exposé in the *Weekend Australian* (28-29 April

---

[121] "Carr takes Abbott to task on Anglo outlook", *Weekend Australian*, 28-29 July 2012, *The Nation*, p. 6.

[122] Phillip Adams, "Wrecking crews", *Weekend Australian*, 4-5 Aug. 2012, Life & Style, p. 46.

[123] Jane Cadzow, "Cape crusader", *SMH*, 25 Aug. 2012, Good Weekend, pp. 12-17.

2012[124]). The emphasis was more on the fact that Pearson had abused a female journalist and done so with language "so foul it couldn't be repeated here". However, Koch was able to report Pearson's lesser abuse of calling government officials and another female journalist "f**king racist white c***s".

Despite this behaviour Pearson claims to be philosophically opposed to the concept of race, especially in governmental policy. In this view the British content of Australia's national identity is all cultural. Likewise, Aboriginal identity and disability have nothing to do with race.[125] The National Trust of Australia has named Pearson a living national treasure, something of a contrast to the treatment afforded whites who deploy vulgar racial abuse. Professor Marcia Langton, foundation chair of Australian indigenous studies at Melbourne University, defended Pearson's harsh language by describing it as a feature of Aboriginal English, in which profanities are used as emphatics, "like exclamation marks". Langton did not insert a sunset clause in her argument, such as a proviso that the cultural excuse expires in the case of a speaker who has a law degree or exercises political and administrative leadership. The twilight of Langton's argument was when she herself lapsed into vilification by referring to "[t]he Anglo preference for supercilious politeness". The comment was published without apology by the *Weekend Australian* (5-6 May 2012[126]).

Also excused were negative views about whites expressed by Gracelyn Smallwood, an Aboriginal activist and an associate professor at James Cook University, made in the context of criticising Pearson. Smallwood made invidious generalisations

---

[124]   Tony Koch, "Pearson yet to learn lessons of leadership", *Weekend Australian*, 28-29 April, Inquirer, p. 18.

[125]   Noel Pearson, "Constitutional reform crucial to indigenous wellbeing", *Weekend Australian*, 24-25 Dec. 2012, Inquirer, p. 20.

[126]   Marcia Langton, "Why I continue to be inspired by Pearson", *Weekend Australian*, 5-6 May 2012, Inquirer, p. 20.

about Anglos and whites in the *Weekend Australian* of 7-8 July 2012.[127] She wrote that white Australians prefer Noel Pearson's approach to indigenous affairs, referred to the "racist realities of mainstream Australia", and opined that Aborigines "have long ago given up hoping that white right-wingers might be capable of understanding such things". She continued that "Anglo-Saxon pride has been promoted for over 200 years in Australian schools. Just because it talks of being fair dinkum doesn't disguise its origins or trajectory."

The treatment of racist language used by Aborigines and their supporters fits the "moral apartheid" described by Herald commentator Paul Sheehan, in which Aborigines are judged by different, lighter, standards,[128] though in the broader picture it seems that the Anglo community is judged harshly in contrast to minorities.

A higher-profile example of anti-Anglo sentiment being excused concerns the late art critic Robert Hughes (1938-2012). Hughes was a prominent expatriate Australian who supported the republican cause in the 1999 referendum from New York, where he was art critic for *Time* magazine (from 1970). His anti-monarchical views extended to criticism of the British core of Australia's national identity. He had unpleasant ethnically-charged memories of Catholic education, expressed in his book *The Culture of Complaint* (1993, p. 89). "Our education would prepare us to be little Englishmen and Englishwomen, though with nasal accents. We would not be accepted as such by the English themselves: we were not up to that. . . . In those days we had a small, 95 percent white, Anglo-Irish society . . . We were taught little Australian history." The sentiment resembles that

---

127 Gracelyn Smallwood, "Self-belief a matter of survival for indigenous people", *SMH*, 7-8 July 2012.

128 Paul Sheehan, "Mundine sentiment missing the mark", *SMH*, 26 April 2012, p. 11. *http://www.smh.com.au/opinion/politics/mundine-sentiment-missing-the-mark-20120425-1xlil.html*, accessed 30 Aug. 2012.

of the journalist John Pilger, who ridiculed Anglo Australia as a "second-hand England" in his 1992 book *A Secret Country*. In his book, Hughes defended the memory of the dead white males who built up most of the Western artistic and philosophical canon. But nowhere did he defend the right of live white people to witness for an identity that still nurtures that civilisation.

Anti-Anglo sentiment is also omitted from recent press coverage of the 1977 murder of anti-drugs campaigner Donald Mackay (*Herald*, 13 July; 14-15 July 2012[129]). The reports failed to mention the ethnic dimension of the crime. A royal commission concluded that a Calabrian Mafia organisation had targeted Mackay, an Anglo Australian. Albert Grassby, a pioneering figure in Australian multiculturalism, had been a close associate of the Mafia leader who ordered Mackay's murder. Grassby had received generous political donations from this individual for many years. Acting on behalf of the Mafia, Grassby subsequently spread the accusation that Mackay's own family had arranged the murder, for which he was successfully sued by Mackay's widow.[130] None of this was mentioned in recent press reports. An elite newspaper can be expected to inform readers of such background, indicating that Mackay's death was an ethnically-entailed conspiracy and cover-up. Despite Grassby's criminal activities having been revealed, the ACT's Labor Government erected a life-sized statue of him, which still stands, a cold display of contempt for the Mackay family, the Anglo community and law abiding citizens.[131]

---

[129] Lisa Davies, "Hopes high in search for remains of Mackay", *SMH*, 13 July 2012, p. 1; Lisa Davies, "Last chance to ease pain of a town and a crusader's family", *SMH*, 14-15 July 2012, p. 15.

[130] *National Observer* (2005): http://www.nationalobserver.net/2005_winter_ed1.htm, accessed 30 Aug. 2012.

[131] Paul Sheehan, "Monuments to honesty and deceit", *SMH*, 16 Feb. 2009, http://www.smh.com.au/opinion/monuments-to-honesty-and-deceit-20090215-881s.html, accessed 30 Aug. 2012.

Of the foregoing media reports, two of the largest categories are contradictory. Whites are commonly depicted abusing and stereotyping non-whites but also common is actual abuse and stereotyping of Anglos. No examples were sighted of journalists or commentators defaming minorities. Such behaviour exists but it is rare in the mainstream media, where abuse of Anglo Australia is common. The asymmetry in pecks and the identity and institutional affiliations of the peckers indicates that Australia has an ethnic hierarchy in which Anglos are firmly underneath and an alliance of leftist intellectuals and minorities are firmly on top. The examples also indicate that the hierarchy is not the natural order of things but is maintained through soft totalitarianism, known euphemistically as "political correctness", consisting of intolerance on the part of the elite media, lack of political alternatives, and intimidation both informal and formal delivered by a growingly authoritarian and openly anti-Anglo immigration industry.

The low status of Anglo advocacy

The media review also revealed a pronounced status difference in Australian ethnic relations. Ethnic minorities are routinely represented by university-educated elites with access to the mass media and government while the ethnic majority is usually not. Rare exceptions, such as Professor Geoffrey Blainey was perceived to be in the 1980s, prove the rule, as does the fury they provoke from the mainstream media and left activists. The class difference corresponds with institutional support, such that minority advocates are privileged by the establishment while majority advocates are excluded from and sanctioned by it. Minority ethnic activists are treated with respect by government, the media, universities, and corporations. They receive positive media coverage, jobs and other perks from the immigration industry. They are invited to participate in government forums. Political parties sometimes favour them for preselection as a means of attracting the "ethnic vote". Activist lawyers volunteer strategy and legal services. Peccadilloes and indiscretions are overlooked. By contrast, majority activists are derided by the media, university experts, minority activists, and government officials. There are no jobs for advocates of Anglo-Australian interests in the multicultural industry or in government agencies. They are not invited to government forums. Lawyers demand full payment. Majority advocacy can stunt careers. Peccadilloes and indiscretions become the whole story. Throughout the West efforts continue to legislate ever harsher penalties for expressions of loyalty to shrinking white majorities.

Vilification of Anglo ethnic consciousness helps perpetuate this difference. The resulting stigma helps silence the professional class that could marshal a powerful electoral and cultural defence of the historical nation.

The class difference between minority and majority ethnic advocates may have been instrumental in the top-down demographic revolution now underway across the English-speaking world. This can happen in a democracy when elites become alienated from the founding nation. According to the best academic study of the phenomenon in the U.S., by Canadian sociologist Eric Kaufmann, by 1950 Anglo elites were stepping away from their traditional role of national leadership.[132] Kaufmann argues that this change of heart occurred initially in the upper echelons of the intellectual elite, largely due to leftist ideologues such as Boas driving Anglo loyalists out of the social sciences and literary circles. (The remainder of this synopsis drops the positive spin Kaufmann puts on cosmopolitanism.)

One of the first casualties was consideration of human nature, the scientific study of which offered a prestigious counterweight

---

[132] Kaufmann, *The rise and fall of Anglo-America*.

to millenarian socialism. This changing of the intellectual guard occurred in the United States by the 1940s and was already apparent in the 1920s and 1930s with the rise of anti-Anglo ideology dressed up as anti-racism. That was the tipping point. The Gramscian process came full circle as graduates of elite universities conveyed the cosmopolitan agenda to the federal government, including the executive, the Supreme Court, and senior levels of the bureaucracy. The alienation of the state from the nation left the latter without effective leadership and thus ill-equipped institutionally or financially to contest control of centralised government, education, and media.

Unable to fight back at the elite level, the remainder of the 20th century saw the mopping-up of uncoordinated pockets of Anglo dissent. One rearguard action was flight from the mainstream churches to evangelical denominations whose preachers were not the products of Ivy League colleges or adherents of progressive ecumenicalism. Despite such resistance, the top-down march of cosmopolitan ideas had a general indoctrination effect. The ability of Anglo Americans to resist electorally was steadily eroded by the mass immigration of those whose ethnic and economic interests usually lay with the Democrats, the party of relatively generous welfare, diversity enthusiasm and porous borders. Coercive measures were also deployed, formal and informal, that characterise multiculturalism everywhere (though in America the First Amendment guaranteeing freedom of speech has been a stumbling block to criminalising racial vilification). This was a repeat of the intolerance originally shown by the left in the elite universities. Kaufmann is critical of the anti-Anglo stance of multiculturalism, suggesting that this endangers the cosmopolitan enterprise.[133]

The process is similar in Australia, though a greater proportion of the intellectual influence has come from overseas. The Anglo elite was becoming alienated from ethnic defence by the 1960s.

---

[133] *Ibid.*, pp. 293, 295.

The Immigration Reform Group, founded in 1960 at Melbourne University, was influential in advocating ethnic moralism that soared unburdened by a concept of ethnic interests. Loyalists have still not found a response to their people's loss of control over the state. From the 1960s the universities became a stronghold for anti-Anglo activists, eventually leading to school curricula having their civics courses stripped of patriotic history. The present Labor government is intent on introducing a national civics curriculum for schools that teaches children nothing of the country's Anglo-Celtic and European history. Instead it intends to emphasise Aboriginal culture, Asian geography, environmental sustainability, and leftist values.[134] As Christ Berg of the Institute of Public Affairs notes, Australia's own English and European political traditions are not mentioned in the draft curriculum; neither is individual liberty. And as the Australian Christian Lobby argues, there is no justification for ignoring Western biblical traditions.[135]

The potential for shifting demographics to prevent an Anglo recovery was demonstrated during the 2007 federal election, when the serving prime minister, John Howard, lost his seat to a campaign that pulled Asian votes from him on the basis of ethnic affiliation. One comment that he made twenty years earlier, to the effect that Asian immigration should be slowed a little during times of economic recession, a view he later withdrew, was sufficient to convince conservative middle class voters of Asian origin to support the party of the left.[136] Race trumped class. More significantly, the commentariat did not hurl accusations of racism at the Labor Party or ethnically-motivated voters. Instead they commended the tactics used. It seems that anti-racism does sometimes mean anti-white. The

---

[134] "New civics curriculum calls for students to be citizens of the web", *SMH*, 5 June 2012, p. 3.

[135] Christ Berg, "Blatant bias in national curriculum could damage our democracy", *Sun-Herald*, 8 July 2012, pp. 68-9. ACL submission on the national curriculum, 28 May 2010.

foregoing examples of media defamation send the same message. A similar double standard prevents the Greens from opposing mass immigration, which transforms low-polluting Third Worlders into the highest polluters on the planet, overnight. In a way, race trumps the environment.

The subordination and steady replacement of Anglo Australia is not due to high principle but an unholy left-minority alliance. The cosmopolitan left has abandoned the shrinking white blue collar working class for new constituencies, including minority ethnics who can be relied upon to vote for parties that keep the immigration door open to ethnic kin. Australia's leftist elites are, in effect, electing a new people to replace reactionary Anglo Australia. The fact that the new peoples are more ethnically motivated than Anglo Australians has not bothered ideologues who are on hair trigger alert for any hint of Anglo ethnic sentiment.

The next chapter describes how the national question is treated in Australia's universities. Are the confusion, double standards and outright anti-white hostility evident in the media occurring despite or because of what is being taught in the social sciences?

---

[136] Maxine McKew, who defeated Howard in the 2007 elections, won partly because the Labor machine targeted the Asian vote: *http://www.smh.com.au/articles/2007/12/12/1197135558234.html*, accessed 1 Sept. 2012; see supporting comments by Asian community leaders in the Bennelong electorate: *http://www.abc.net.au/news/stories/2010/08/20/2988368.htm?site=sydney*, accessed 1 Sept. 2012.

Australia and the National Question Part II: The Universities

In the previous chapter I reviewed elements of the quality media, mainly the *Sydney Morning Herald* and intermittently the ABC and SBS, for one year, from mid September 2011 to August 2012. These media outlets represent the apogee of respectable, mainstream left-liberal ideology in Australia, ostensibly the heart of sophisticated cosmopolitanism, what the elite read and watch. I found confused understandings of ethnic behaviour, numerous incidents of baiting and defamation of Anglo and white Australians, but no chauvinism directed at minority ethnic groups. The search was not exhaustive but the trend is unlikely to be altered by a few missed cases running in the opposite direction. Neither is the trend altered by articles that report unpleasant facts about minorities in a dispassionate manner. An example is a 2010 article by conservative columnist Andrew Bolt in the Melbourne *Herald-Sun*, a Murdoch-owned newspaper.[137] Bolt criticised the Victorian Police for suppressing information on the ethnicity of criminals and stated some statistics showing high rates of imprisonment for some immigrant groups. He did not use terms of abuse such as those directed at Anglos and whites in the *Herald*.

---

[137] Andrew Bolt (2010). Tell truth on ethnic crime. *Herald-Sun*, 19 March. *http://www.heraldsun.com.au/opinion/tell-truth-on-ethnic-crime/story-e6frfhqf-1225842538542*, accessed 26 Sept. 2012.

Spread over twelve months, the hostility shown towards Anglo Australians occurred at a moderate frequency. Viewed in isolation it was not out of place. Some ethnic and ideological sniping is normal and to be expected. Remarkable was the near total lack of similar abuse directed at minorities in the quality media and an absence of warmth towards Anglo Australians identified as such. Clearly the latter do not enjoy the immunity from defamation bestowed on migrant and indigenous communities. The review revealed a hierarchy of regard with Anglos and whites in the subordinate position.

In this chapter I examine the contribution of Australia's universities to public culture regarding the national question. There was little evidence in the media I reviewed of academics stepping in to correct the anti-white bias and theoretical confusion. Could it be that the relevant knowledge is scarce in Australian universities, at least in the social sciences?

Indirect evidence that the ghost of Franz Boas still haunts the antipodean ivory tower comes from leading scholars of ethnicity and nationalism who I contacted. They could not name one Australian scholar who professes biosocial theory. This is in line with the survey reported in the first essay in this series.[138] No political science or sociology department reported a scholar basing his or her research or teaching on behavioural biology. The skew towards Marxist and other environmental theories means that scholars of nationality do not know what to do with the wealth of findings drawn from evolutionary psychology, ethology, and sociobiology; except ignore them.

Further evidence comes from a recent student in a leading university studying nationalism, who reports that the approach was heavily Marxist. In the first year his course consisted of one

---

[138]   Salter, F. K. (2012). "The war against human nature in the social sciences." *Quadrant* 56(6 (487)): 49-57.
http://www.quadrant.org.au/magazine/issue/2012/6/the-war-against-human-nature-in-the-social-sciences

week covering supposedly primordial theory and thirteen weeks of the usual fare. The core texts were Benedict Anderson's *Imagined Communities* and Eric Hobsbawm's *Nations and Nationalism Since 1780*. I have also drawn on these texts as teaching material. But they need to be treated critically because both are radically constructionist. Both argue that ethnicities and nations are socially constructed, not based on realities of genetic and cultural similarity. Hobsbawm is a Marxist at the London School of Economics who emphasises the recency of ethnic traditions and whose formulaic dismissal of behavioural biology allows him to downplay primordial origins.

The interesting development among LSE ethnic theorists has come from the circle around Anthony D. Smith and Australian John Hutchinson and other scholars such as Walker Connor in the U.S. Their comparative approach and theory of ethno-symbolism allows for behavioural and genetic factors to be introduced to the analysis. Unlike radical theorists they do not criticise Western societies as notably egregious. Smith's seminal contribution has been to show that nation states develop around ancient ethnic cores.[139] When clarified in biosocial perspective by theorists such as Walker Connor and J. Philippe Rushton[140] this finding contradicts the view that nations represent ideals or are secondary effects of class processes.

The latter fallacy is commonplace in Austalia's political culture. For example, a *Herald* editorial implied that the Australian Secret Intelligence Service's mission is to stop the enemies of the open society. That would be a congenial outcome but is not its prime mission, which is to defend the Australian nation, whatever its present economic or social system. The great Enoch Powell made this point in debate with Margaret Thatcher

---

[139] Smith, A. D. (1986). *The ethnic origins of nations*. Oxford, Basil Blackwell.

[140] Connor, W. (1993). "Beyond reason: The nature of the ethnonational bond." *Ethnic and Racial Studies* 16(3): 373-389.
Rushton, J. P. (2005). "Ethnic nationalism".

shortly before the Falklands War. The prime minister said that a strong defence force was needed to protect Western values.

Powell: 'No, we do not fight for values. I would fight for this country even if it had a communist government.' Thatcher: 'Nonsense, Enoch. If I send British troops abroad, it will be to defend our values.' 'No, Prime Minister, values exist in a transcendental realm, beyond space and time. They can neither be fought for, nor destroyed.' Mrs Thatcher looked utterly baffled. She had just been presented with the difference between Toryism and American Republicanism.[141]

Consistent with Powell's distinction is the hierarchy of bonds. People are more likely to sacrifice for their nations than for abstract principles.[142] The nation is the largest secular entity able to elicit robust solidarity.

Implicit anti-white bias also contributes to the unbalanced analysis of the national question. A frequent approach is to treat Anglo ethnicity mainly as a risk factor for racism, but immigrant ethnicity as a legitimate and rich human value. Consider the immigration expert consulted by the *Herald* journalist who criticised the anti-Islamic activist cited in the first part of this article.[143] Professor Kevin Dunn is Head of School of Human Geography and Urban Studies at the University of Western Sydney (UWS). His reported comments were critical of anti-diversity and anti-Muslim views. Did the *Herald* journalist omit reporting comments sympathetic to Anglo concerns as normal in the circumstances? Professor Dunn's publication list indicates not, and is a window into the

---

[141] *http://en.wikipedia.org/wiki/Enoch_Powell#cite_note-39*, accessed 27 Aug. 2012.

[142] Salter, F. K. (2002). "Ethnic nepotism as a two-edged sword: The risk-mitigating role of ethnicity among mafiosi, nationalist fighters, middlemen, and dissidents." In *Risky transactions. Kinship, ethnicity, and trust.* F. K. Salter (ed.). Oxford and New York, Berghahn: 243-289.

[143] *SMH*, 21 Aug. 2012, p. 3.

world of academic multiculturalism.[144] His research is funded by the academic and multicultural establishments.[145]

Professor Dunn's website lists 46 publications and research projects, 20 dealing directly with racism and ethnic discrimination. Going by article titles and available abstracts, none study these phenomena in non-whites or Muslims. None study Anglo or white interests or victimhood. None indicate reliance on human universals or behavioural biology, while several claim a constructivist approach. Several do study Muslims' and other immigrant groups' experience of hostility, which is categorised as a phobia, implying groundless or excessive fear.[146] Several investigate Anglos' denial of their own racism and privilege. Anglo racism, privilege and immigrant victimhood are treated as axiomatic. For example, the "new racism" is held to be a distinctively Anglo view of the nation as assimilationist, ethnocultural, or egalitarian, a narrow conception at odds with the civic nationalism on which multiculturalism is based.[147] Egalitarian images of Australia are a form of Anglo racism, it is argued, because they deny the supposed reality of Anglo privilege.[148] One paper published in

---

[144] *http://www.uws.edu.au/ssap/school_of_social_sciences_and_psychology/ key_people/academic_staff_directory/kevin_dunn*, accessed 27 Aug. 2012.

[145] Nine of Kevin Dunn's projects have received grants, mostly on racism and multicultural themes. Six were supported by the Australian Research Council (ARC), Australia's peak research funding body. Two were funded by the Australian Human Rights and Equal Opportunity Commission (HREOC) in collaboration with similar bodies working at the state level. One was funded by the Department of Immigration and Citizenship. One study, of "Intolerance and Discrimination towards Minority Cultural Groups in Victoria" was funded by the Victorian Health Promotion Foundation, in 2006-7.

[146] E.g. See the abstract of Dunn et al. (2007). "Contemporary racism and Islamaphobia in Australia: Racialising religion", Ethnicities, 7(4): 564-89. *http://etn.sagepub.com/content/7/4/564.abstract*, accessed 25 Sept. 2012.

[147] J. Forrest and K. Dunn, 2006, "Racism and intolerance in Eastern Australia: A geographic perspective", *Australian Geographer*, 37(2): 167-86. *http://www.tandfonline.com/doi/abs/10.1080/00049180600711082*, accessed 25 Sept. 2012.

2011[149] reports survey data indicating that Australians of non-Anglo background were "significantly more likely than those from Anglo backgrounds and Australian-born respondents to deny that racial prejudice exists in Australia". The paper interprets this as evidence of a pathology in Australian society in which subordinate ethnicities are discouraged from admitting that they suffer from racism. An alternative interpretation was apparently not considered, that immigrants simply encounter low levels of discrimination.

Racial Discrimination Commissioner Helen Szoke's hostile attitude towards Anglo Australia, discussed in the first part of this article, begins to look normal when compared with mainstream academic analysis. It is easy to find prominent academics whose writing on ethnicity promotes the transformation of Australia through immigration, shows a cold indifference to the Australian nation, and affords no place for human nature.

An example is a 2011 paper on Australia-Chinese relations and its implications for Australian politics, by Andrew Jakubowicz, Professor of Sociology at the University of Technology Sydney. Jakubowicz was foundation director of the Centre for Multicultural Studies at Wollongong University and collaborated with the Office of the Board of Studies of NSW to produce the award-winning website *Making Multicultural Australia in the 21st Century*. The website is aimed at school pupils. The paper[150] assembles important information about Chinese ethnic activism in Australia, beginning with the

---

[148] K. Dunn et al. (2004). "Constructing racism in Australia". *The Australian Journal of Social Issues*, 39(4).
http://search.informit.com.au/documentSummary;dn=937672105564037;res=IEL HSS, accessed 25 Sept. 2012.

[149] *http://www.tandfonline.com/doi/abs/10.1080/07256868.2011.618105*, accessed 27 Aug. 2012.

[150] Jakubowicz, A. (2011). "Empires of the Sun: Towards a post-multicultural Australian politics." *Cosmopolitan Civil Societies Journal* 3(1): 65-85.

unseating of John Howard in the 2007 federal elections. It describes how Chinese-Australian influence is based on strong representation in some professions and business sectors, on large targeted donations to political parties, and on international linkages mobilised by pan-Chinese nationalism. The Chinese community does not present a united front in advancing its interest, but Jakubowicz expects such a front to develop because "a multicultural policy depends on well-organised ethnically-focused organisations able to both articulate interests of their groups, and engage in coalitions with similar groups to deliver broader policy outcomes that provide individual benefits to the groups, and to their constituencies" (p. 78).

The analysis then takes an ethnocentric turn. Instead of canvassing strategies Australia might adopt to protect its interests against a diaspora with ethnic ties to a nearby rising power, Jakubowitz constructs a brief for ethnic Chinese grievance against alleged white Australian racism. Citing Kevin Dunn among others, he states that the "Australian political system is still influenced by racist histories, while Asian immigrants still experience some forms of racism" (p. 79). He states that racism has been a defining characteristic of the Australian nation and has not dissipated. Traditional Chinese ethnocentrism is not discussed. He mocks past concerns about Chinese invasion and declares the need to finally break down white racism in order to allow Chinese ethnics, in unspecified numbers, full participation in national identity and governance. Australia's challenge, Zakubowicz argues, is finally to expunge its racialised state structure. The bitter legacy of Blainey and Howard must be buried and Chinese-Australian history made an integral part of the emerging Australian ethno-nationalist narrative (p. 81).

Jakubowicz commits some fallacies and emits some hostilities that resemble those found in the elite media. He simultaneously calls for minorities to organise ethnically to advance their corporate interests and condemns white Australians for any hint of doing the same. Evidence of white discrimination against Asians is not compared with data on Asian discrimination, for example the renowned success of cohesive Chinese middleman trading networks in dominating markets throughout Southeast Asia.[151] In this view whites have no legitimate ethnic interests. Their only ethical option is complete acquiescence to minority demands, which represent bountiful legitimate group interests. Another consequence is that the call for Chinese-Australian participation in a reconstructed Australian nation is unrestrained by numbers. This is typical of multicultural ideology, that it allows for displacement of Western populations. The failure to discuss the numbers issue also reflects a cavalier attitude towards Australian security in light of Jakubowicz's acknowledgement of the growth of pan-Chinese nationalism and its linkage to China's economic and military power. These potential threats could be channelled by ethnic Chinese representation in Australian politics and business. A final fallacy is acceptance of Foucaultian constructionist theory unrestrained by human nature, which allows the fantasy that manipulation of Australia's national historical narrative can produce something that has never existed, a diverse ethno-nation possessing the same benefits of social cohesion, social capital and allegiance that accrue to real nations. It is doubtful that Chinese-Australian interests would be served by allowing themselves to become allied with the grievance industry,[152] though this might advance Chinese regional hegemony.

Radical anti-Western analysis of race and nation is not new. Consider the book *Mistaken Identity: Multiculturalism and the*

---

[151]   Chua, A. (2003). *World on fire: How exporting free market democracy breeds ethnic hatred and global instability.* Doubleday.

[152]   Keith Windschuttle, "Chronicle", *Quadrant*, October 2011. *http://www.quadrant.org.au/magazine/issue/2011/10/keith-windschuttle.*

Demise of Nationalism in Australia, (1988),[153] by Stephen Castles and colleagues, assumes that Western societies have been inherently racist, including Australia, Western Europe and of course the United States. The racism concept is used promiscuously. At a formal level the book defines it to include emotional ties, and even criticises the "racism" of ethnic minorities who stick together. But 'racism' is mainly used to convey the colloquial meaning of ethnic prejudice and hatred and is thus a term of opprobrium. This mixed meaning has helped make 'racism' useful to social critics but next to worthless for serious analysis. On the one hand it is used reasonably to describe categorical hostility towards a racial group but the same word is applied to liberal-democratic polities such as France and Germany in the 1970s. Australia is especially condemnable, the authors contend, because for much of the country's history racism has been used in an attempt to increase social cohesion. They describe historian Geoffrey Blainey's 1984 criticism of high levels of Asian immigration on the ground that it threatened social stability as "an attempt to develop an embracing racist ideology". One meaning not given to racism is defence of ethnic group interests or other adaptive functions. Overly liberal application of the racism concept obscures the distinction between ethnicity and race. Thus the authors claim that in 1992 Australia could not adopt the "racist" strategy of reaffirming its historical British identity because, in that year, only three quarters of the population were of British descent. But Britishness is an ethnic category, not a racial one. The white racial category in 1992 was much greater than 75 percent of the Australian population.

In arguing for a socialist form of multiculturalism that eliminates group inequality, *Mistaken Identity* does not countenance ethnic differences in economic behaviour. Without

---

[153] Castles, S., B. Cope, M. Kalantzis, and M. Morrissey (1992). *Mistaken identity: Multiculturalism and the demise of nationalism in Australia*. Sydney, Pluto Press, pp. 139-48.

entertaining such differences, inequality can only be due to oppression or bad luck, which makes radical social engineering seem more appropriate. This leftist myth is still mainstream in the social sciences. For example, well into the 21st century university courses in politics and sociology still do not cover group differences in IQ, a strong predictor of educational success and social mobility.[154] Greater weight is given to the mythical agency of white racism in producing inequality, setting the stage for Castles and co-authors' conclusion: "Above all, the history of white racism and genocide against the Aborigines must become a central theme of education and public debate, and an accommodation with the Aborigines must be achieved through payment of reparations and Land Rights legislation." They add that Australia's social organisation must be redefined to deemphasise the nation state because the national idea conflicts with the projects of abolishing white racism and maximising diversity.

Mistaken Identity suffers from the attempt to combine empirical analysis with agit-prop stirring. Factors and analytically useful concepts that conflict with the policy agenda are simply omitted. Nevertheless, or perhaps consequently, the book has been remarkably influential. Issued in three editions (1988, 1990 and 1992), many of its recommendations have been accomplished or are proposed, such as the present Labor government's attempt to remove the last vestiges of Western history and Anglo identity from the national civics curriculum.

The book has not hurt its authors' careers. Consider the lead author. Stephen Castles has impeccable globalist credentials. He is a sociologist and political economist specialising in

---

[154] Gottfredson, L. S. (1997). "Why *g* matters: The complexity of everyday life." *Intelligence* 24(1): 79-132.
Lynn, R. and T. Vanhanen (2002). *IQ and the wealth of nations*. Westport, Conn., Praeger.
Lynn, R. and T. Vanhanen (2006). *IQ and global inequality*. Augusts, Georgia, Washington Summit Publishers.

international migration and its transformatory effects. He has advised the British and Australian governments and has worked for the International Labour Organisation, the International Organisation for Migration, the European Union and other international organisations. He is presently Research Chair in Sociology at Sydney University. Earlier in his career, at Wollongong University, he was Director of the Centre for Asia Pacific Social Transformation Studies and, like Andrew Jakubowicz, Director of the Centre for Multicultural Studies (1986-1996).[155] The second author, Bill Cope, was also at the Centre (1984-1991) and was the Australian Federal Government's First Assistant Secretary and Director of the Office of Multicultural Affairs in the *Department of the Prime Minister and Cabinet* (1995-6), when he was also Director of the Bureau of Immigration, Multicultural and Population Research in the Department of Immigration and Multicultural Affairs, and presently Professor of Education Policy at the University of Illinois, Urbana-Champaign. The third author, Mary Kalantzis has also had a successful academic career and served as Commissioner of the Australian Human Rights and Equal Opportunity Commission and as Chair of the Queensland Ethnic Affairs Ministerial Advisory Committee. The radicals advocating the deconstruction of Western societies are not shouting in the streets at the establishment. By the 1990s they were in the establishment.

An extreme example of the politicisation of the field of ethnic studies is the school of "whiteness studies". This began with a Marxist thesis developed in the well-known book *The Wages of Whiteness* (1999) by American historian David Roediger. The thesis is that belonging to the white race brings unearned social and economic advantages. This is perhaps the theoretical basis for the claim that Anglo Australians are privileged. Australia

---

[155] *http://sydney.edu.au/arts/sociology_social_policy/staff/profiles/ stephen_castles.shtml*, accessed 20 Sept. 2012.

has its own academic whiteness studies association, The Australian Critical Race and Whiteness Studies Association (ACRAWSA),[156] whose goal is to "[c]ritically investigate and challenge racial privilege and the construction and maintenance of race and whiteness . . .". A political agenda is evident in the failure to generalise the thesis. Do not members of other ethnicities and races benefit from group membership? Are there not wages of blackness or of Chineseness? Why are there only benefits for whites and disadvantages for non-whites? The school does not attempt to assess the costs of whiteness, such as affirmative action, at a time when the white man's burden weighs heavily upon him. White societies around the world are in steep demographic and economic decline, a fact not easy to reconcile with the unchanging white hegemony alleged in whiteness studies. The sole emphasis on white privilege, in a diverse world in which that race is in headlong retreat, is difficult to distinguish from racial animus.

Another analytical flaw is the school's dogma that race is a social construct, that it has no objective existence. The notion is found throughout the social sciences and humanities. Also absent from whiteness studies is the concept of ethnic interests, a recurring deficiency of contemporary ethnic studies.

Left radicalism does not monopolise academic ethnic studies in Australia. An example of moderate liberal analysis, though still lacking a biosocial dimension, is that of David Brown at Murdoch University. Brown analyses multiculturalism as a form of corporatism that privileges minority communities. The effect, he argues, has been to withdraw state support from the majority and instead re-educate it in the "virtues and advantages of ethnic pluralism".[157] Another invidious consequence has been that the majority are "portrayed as the

---

[156] ACRAWSA's website is at http://www.acrawsa.org.au/about/

[157] David Brown (2000). *Contemporary nationalism. Civic, ethnocultural and multicultural politics*. London, Routledge, p. 139.

ethnic community whose previous dominance must now be compensated for by their new subordination".[158] Thus Australian multiculturalism has turned the state against the Anglo-Celtic majority, in contrast to the type of multiculturalism adopted in Singapore in which all ethnic groups, including the Chinese majority, receive corporate protection from the state.[159] Brown implies that what is being done to Anglo-Celtic Australians is unjust and also dangerous because states that exclude the majority from consideration are more likely "to face the . . . electorally destabilising wrath of the ethnic majority".[160] He advocates individual-pluralist amelioration of ethnic diversity in which the state does not favour any side. The shortcoming of pluralism is that it pretends that all ethnicities are equal, putting the historical Anglo-Celtic nation on an equal footing with numerous immigrant groups. By not acknowledging and analysing ethnic group interests, pluralism would perpetuate the alienation of the state from the culture that established it.

The subjects of ethnicity and race are recurring weaknesses of social science stripped of behavioural biology. Academics and media commentators are frequently unsure of what these concepts mean and how they interact. This became evident in the controversy and court case concerning commentator Andrew Bolt.

Bolt expressed skepticism about the genuineness of Aboriginal identity on the part of individuals who lack visible racial characteristics.[161] He was sued by nine individuals who objected that although they were light skinned they identified with those ancestors who were indigenous and were hurt, humiliated and

[158] Brown, p. 132.

[159] Brown, pp. 139-41.

[160] Brown, p. 141.

[161] Bolt, A. (2009). It's so hip to be black. *Herald-Sun*. Melbourne, News Ltd.

offended by Bolt's remarks. On 28th September 2011 the suit was upheld and Bolt was found to have contravened section 18C of the Racial Discrimination Act, though he had not been antagonistic to any race. His crime was not so much assuming that subjective identification necessary follows the weight of ancestry, but his application to self-declared Aborigines of a type of mockery that is usually reserved for white advocates: that their emphasis of ethnicity is extreme and divisive.

The guilty verdict was criticised by conservative commentators on the grounds that it impinged on freedom of speech. Bolt can also be defended on empirical grounds, though the evidence does not all go his way. It is true that indigenous identity can be felt by individuals who lack distinctive Aboriginal racial characteristics. But race can be a salient ethnic marker. Religion, language, dress and other cultural characteristics can mark ethnicity. But racial difference is important to external judgments of ethnicity because it is genetically caused and therefore persistent as an identity marker even after full cultural assimilation. And racial differences are visible at a distance. In mass anonymous societies appearance is the only information available about most people we encounter in public places. The language, religion, diet, personality and political views of those comprising a crowd might be invisible but their racial makeup is obvious on cursory inspection.

Race is also a marker of descent, though it does not distinguish between populations of the same race. Difference of race signals at least some difference of ancestry, and at the heart of ethnic group feeling is the belief that the group shares ancestors. Surely it is significant that an individual of indigenous racial appearance is more likely to be perceived to be Aboriginal than one who looks white? A recurring theme in ethnic studies is someone "passing" for one ethnicity despite being descended from another, and the effect this has on status and social options.

Racial appearance can also complicate subjective identification. For a number of reasons individuals of mixed ancestry can identify with one set of ancestors more than another. As a result, hybridity does not remove race as a variable. A prominent example is U.S. president Barack Obama who has a black African father and white mother. Despite being raised by his mother's family and half his genetic inheritance being European, his ethnic identity tracked his African racial appearance. He devoted his post-Harvard career to advocating the interests of African Americans.

Another factor that connects race and ethnicity is genetic similarity, which at the population level is highest within racially marked ethnic groups. Similarity of ethnicity draws people together in marriages, friendships, and networks, producing pockets of relative ethnic and racial homogeneity.[162] A result of this universal tendency to implicit ethnicity is that the overwhelming majority of ethnically and racially discriminatory acts are normal and morally neutral. The analytical challenge is to define the small subset that deserves condemnation, for example as "racism". Criteria include contractual obligations and compassion but a useful definition cannot encompass universal adaptive choices. Ethnic solidarity can be adaptive because ethnic groups typically have different genetic interests, in the same way that families do but at a scale several orders of magnitude greater. A racial component to ethnic difference magnifies this effect. It seems that few if any in Australian social science departments have taken on board the fact that ethnic genetic kinship is real, has been measured and is substantial. I could find only one biosocial treatment of

---

[162] McPherson, M., L. Smith-Lovin, et al. (2001). Birds of a feather: Homophily in social networks. *Annual Review of Sociology*. K. S. Cook and J. Hagan. Palo Alto, California, *Annual Review*. 27: 415-444.
Rushton, J. P. (2005). "Ethnic nationalism, evolutionary psychology, and genetic similarity theory." *Nations and Nationalism* 11: 489-507.

ethnicity or nationality in an Australian journal, and that was by me in 2008.[163]

The left-multicultural approach to ethnic conflict dates to the early twentieth century in the United States and was a mature thread of the cosmopolitan critique of the West by the 1960s, for example in E. Digby Baltzell's classic denunciation of Wasp ethnicity, *The Protestant Establishment: Aristocracy and Caste in America* (1964). Baltzell treated Anglos as possessing no legitimate interests that might be threatened by other ethnic groups and thus by mass immigration. He clinically examined Anglo-Americans, and only Anglo-Americans, for any sign of ethnic solidarity, inevitably finding symptoms which he promptly diagnosed as immoral. He treated immigrant communities very differently, as possessing legitimate interests that are often threatened by Anglo racism but which would be wholly benign if realised. In this perspective minorities harbour no competitive ethnic sentiments, a most improbable exception from human nature.

Biosocial analysis of the national question is less likely to get bogged down by ethnic or ideological loyalties because from the biological perspective all populations share the same interest in survival, status and resources. Science is not judgmental. There is much left to discover but the needed research orientation appears to be rare in Australian social science departments, the result of the West losing the cold war over human nature. Promising research topics include: the distinction between the strong force of group identification and the weak but ubiquitous force of similarity-attraction; how this distinction maps onto conscious and subconscious ethnicity; the development of ethnic consciousness from birth and how it sheds light on cultural, genetic, and psychological influences; how the method of live brain scanning is contributing to this knowledge; sex

---

[163] Salter, F. K. (2008). "Evolutionary analyses of ethnic solidarity: An overview." *People and Place* 16(2): 15-25.

differences in ethnic behaviour; the causes of socioeconomic stratification by ethnicity, including group differences in cognitive and personality traits; the evolution of behaviour bearing on ethnicity; group selection and aggregate kinship; slow versus fast life history strategies and ethnic differences; the nature of ethnic interests, proximate and ultimate; social technologies for stabilising ethnically stratified societies; and how all of this can affect political theory, in particular the design of adaptive political systems.

Scientific approaches are also valuable because they break taboos. In the case of ethnicity, one taboo is disloyalty on the part of minorities. This is considered unmentionable but is predictable from biosocial theory. The study of diasporas indicates that Australia's diversity is likely to reduce its degree of consensus in foreign policy and cohesion in times and war. One subject of potential import that is the potential risks posed by Australia's growing population of immigrants whose ethnic homelands are in conflict with Australia. It is predictable that some will feel more moved by ethnic nepotism than attachment to Australia. At present this is true of the Islamic community, as expressed by the Sydney riot of 15 September 2012. An academic Muslim commented in the *Herald* (19 Sept.[164]): "[M]any Muslims in Australia do not simply give up their identity as belonging to a global community merely because they happen to live in Australia. . . . [W]hen a Muslim woman is killed . . . in Afghanistan, these youth are angered at the fact that their sister was murdered. When a Muslim man is crushed to death in Palestine, they lament the loss of their brother."A much greater potential threat comes from diasporas of regional powers. The risk is not sporadic violence but the diplomatic isolation of Australia. The United States is declining economically and its ethnic bond to Australia will weaken as the two countries' become more diverse. At the same time

---

[164] M. Tabbaa, "He's my brother – why angry Muslim youth are protesting in Sydney", *SMH*, 19 Sept. 2012, p. 11.

Australia's Asian population is entering the professions and business class in large numbers, making their loyalty a relevant issue. Some fifth-column activity would be primed by the rise of nationalism in one or more diaspora homelands. Such activity could be initiated domestically or in regional homelands. Australia's diversity is often praised for its vibrancy. It is also a potential asset to regional powers in attempts to separate Australia from its traditional ally.

Who else might the *Herald* journalist have contacted to provide a comment fair to Anglo Australians? Which social scientist would have explained that cultural pride does not somehow become "racial supremacism" when it is felt by white people, or that concern about Sharia law's potential threat to Western secular institutions is not incompatible with the values of modern society? Surely many have that knowledge but are not accessed by the media.

The academic study of ethnicity is hardly a break on the double standards, Anglophobia, and irrationalism of the mainstream media's reporting of ethnic affairs. This represents the victory of radical and anti-Western ideology first expressed by Franz Boas and his school. The deleterious effect on students can be seen in leaders ill-prepared to formulate adaptive policies in immigration and domestic race relations. The left's dogged advocacy of high immigration and multiculturalism despite overwhelming evidence of the anti-social and anti-equality effects of diversity,[165] raises questions about their collective state of mind. Have they taken leave of their senses?

At the minimum they have taken leave of their values by advocating the immigration of cultures that oppose gay rights and equality of women and are far more ethnocentric than Anglos or other Europeans. Bangladeshi-Australian psychiatrist

---

[165] Frank Salter. (2010). "The misguided advocates of open borders." *Quadrant* 54(6). *http://www.quadrant.org.au/magazine/issue/2010/6/the-misguided-advocates-of-open-borders*.

Tanveer Ahmed observed in the *Herald* (26 July[166]) that Chinese and Indian immigrants are conservative and reject most of the social values of those who agitate for open borders. They are eager to vote for conservative parties with the one caveat, Ahmed implies, that those parties pursue the unconservative policy of Asianisation. Ahmed makes clear that that caveat is not motivated by cosmopolitan sentiment. In Australia and America conservative parties that welcome Asian immigration gain the votes of ethnic Indians and Chinese. The priority given to Asian ethnic interests could not be clearer. From this perspective even John Howard was a positive influence, not because he defended religious schools and other conservative causes but because he favoured the ethnic interests of Asians, which includes Dr. Ahmed's own ethnicity. "[I]n spite of John Howard's association with anti-Asian rhetoric, his Liberal government settled more immigrants than any before. It also did more to Asianise our country." Ahmed observes but does not explain the paradox of an Asianisation policy coming from a party that he thought "believe[d] in white Australia and a subservient immigrant class". Nor does he explain the paradox of leftist leaders such as Hawke and Keating abandoning white Australia, with its weak ethnocentrism, and embracing the immigration of relatively intense ethnocentric cultures. A partial explanation comes from sociologist Katharine Betts who observes that the greatest ideological distance between political leaders and followers is in the Labor, Greens and Democrats parties. In explanation she surmises that voters retain some national loyalty while elites have adopted international cosmopolitanism.[167] In effect the anti-Anglo left, by having elements of its agenda embraced by the mainstream parties and the self-serving immigration industry, is succeeding in electing a new population which is far more tribal than the

---

[166] Tanveer Ahmed, *SMH* 26 July 2012, p. 11.

[167] Betts, K. (2004). "People and parliamentarians: The great divide." *People and Place* 12(2): 64-83, p. 79.

old. Something does not add up. Whatever it is that induces both sides of politics to suspend core values in situations where those values would benefit Anglo interests, it is not consistent with white hegemony or even white equality in multicultural Australia. Disinterested anti-racism would assume that the cause is hatred of Anglo Australia, which is consistent with the fealty to minority interests. A biosocial analysis – or a behaviourally-based sociological one – would search for more fundamental causes, such as competitive motives derived from conflicts of ethnic interests.[168]

The origins of Anglo and European intellectual self hatred are obscure. George Orwell remarked that sentiment in English leftist intellectuals in the 1930s. In an essay, "The Lion and the Unicorn: Socialism and the English Genius", published in 1941, he criticised most left intellectuals for lack of patriotism. Orwell was critical of cosmopolitanism because it discounted the bonds of nation. He was a radical socialist but also loved his country and saw that it was threatened by Soviet and Nazi tyranny. He wrote the essay at a time shortly after Dunkirk when Britain was exposed to German bombing and invasion. The most moving section is titled "England Your England". In it Orwell describes what the English identity meant to him and why national freedom was worth defending. He did not attempt to trace anti-English sentiment to its roots. Anti-Anglo cosmopolitanism was introduced to England as early as 1911, when Franz Boas presented his fresh "findings" about the plasticity of race at the Universal Races Congress held at the University of London.[169] The meeting was organised by the local branch of the Ethical Culture Society founded by Felix Adler, held by Eric Kaufmann to be the first public intellectual to

---

[168]   Baker, D. G. (1978). "Race and power: Comparative approaches to the analysis of race relations." *Ethnic and Racial Studies* 1(3): 316-335.

[169]   Spiller, G., Ed. (1911). *Papers on Inter-racial problems: A record of proceedings of the first Universal Races Congress held at the University of London July 26 to 29, 1911.* London, King and Son.

completely sever the ties of ethnicity to achieve a truly cosmopolitan consciousness.[170]

Another source of anti-Western sentiment was revolutionary Marxism, which conceptualised nationalism and ethnic sentiment as types of false consciousness. Anti-racism was at the heart of communism and was enacted by the Bolsheviks during their cosmopolitan phase up to the Second World War. Like Western multiculturalism, Soviet anti-racism was focused on protecting minorities. The regime directed the widespread killing of the Slavic majority, including the Ukrainian genocide of 1931-2 in which many millions were starved to death. In the 1920s the regime also considered the family to be a byproduct of capitalism.[171] This was consistent with utopian socialist suspicion of parents discriminating in favour of their own children. Soviet meddling with the Russian family was as disastrous as any totalitarian utopian experiment and was withdrawn in the late 1920s. Its experiment with cosmopolitanism ended in 1941 when Stalin, desperate to put spine into the Red Army, called on Russians to fight the "Great Patriotic War".

Though impractical, there is a certain logic to the rejection of nation and family, based on an analogy between national solidarity and nepotism. Both involve allegiance based on biological descent or tribe-like affiliation. And both take precedence to class solidarity. The analogy has proven scientifically fruitful in the form of a sociobiological theory that conceptualises ethnic solidarity as "ethnic nepotism".[172] The

---

[170] Kaufmann, E. (2004). *The rise and fall of Anglo-America*. Cambridge, MA, Harvard University Press, Chapter 5.

[171] Heller, M. (1988). *Cogs in the Soviet Wheel. The formation of Soviet Man*. London, Collins Harvill, p. 200.

[172] van den Berghe, P. L. (1981). *The ethnic phenomenon*. New York, Elsevier. Salter, F. K. (2007). Ethnic nepotism as heuristic: Risky transactions and public altruism. *Handbook of evolutionary psychology*. R. I. M. Dunbar and L. Barrett. Oxford, Oxford University Press: 541-551.

utopian fallacy is to map an ethical argument onto the behavioural analogy, thus: If it is wrong (e.g. racist) to care more for a fellow ethnic than a randomly-chosen human, it must also be wrong to care for one's own child more than a randomly-chosen one. The argument is oddly premised and sequenced. A more realistic rendering goes something like this, setting caveats aside: If it's acceptable or commendable to care especially for one's child it must also be acceptable or commendable to care especially for members of one's ethnic group or indeed any category for which one feels an attachment.

The weight of radical anti-national ideology in Australia is indicated by the pressure put on academics who contradict leftist ethnic policy. In 1984 Geoffrey Blainey was demonised when he identified the double standards of what he called the "immigration industry" in stereotyping Anglo Australia as racist while being routinely discriminatory against the white community and for immigrant communities. "Rarely in the history of the modern world has a nation given such preference to a tiny ethnic minority of its population as the Australian Government has done in the past few years, making that minority the favoured majority in its immigration policy."[173]

A more recent criticism of the left-minority political establishment comes from Bob Birrell, reader in sociology at Monash University. Birrell has been subjected to name-calling from senior colleagues[174] because he is a rare social scientist whose analysis includes the costs of diversity and immigration to national cohesion. He argues that multiculturalism serves the interests of minorities, especially in keeping the immigration doors open to a continual flow of co-ethnics. He implies that

---

[173] Geoffrey Blainey, "Race and debate", *Bureau of Immigration and Population Bulletin* 11: 34-7. *http://www.multiculturalaustralia.edu.au/doc/blainey_1.pdf*

[174] Geoff Maslen, "The devil in the detail", *The Age*, 8 Feb. 2011. *http://www.theage.com.au/national/education/the-devil-in-the-detail-20110207-1ajz1.html*, accessed 1 Sept. 2012.

minority solidarity has been marshalled by leftist politicians to bolster their electoral prospects. For one analysis he drew on the work of American Patrick J. Buchanan in his book, *The Death of the West*.[175] The end result, Buchanan argued, will be the subordination of white populations in their homelands. In February 2012 Buchanan was fired as a senior news analyst by CNBC for similar views.

The most Stalinist example of academic intolerance was reserved for actual advocacy of Anglo ethnic interests. In 2005 Andrew Fraser, associate professor of public law at Macquarie University, criticised the immigration of black Africans on the ground that they commit crime at higher rates than do whites. Fraser was suspended from teaching duties and an article in which he documented his assertion was censored from the Deakin University law journal by the University's vice chancellor after it had passed peer review and been accepted by the editor.[176]

Conclusion: Anglo Australia has been subordinated

Anglo Australians are a subaltern ethnicity. They are second-class citizens, the only ethnic group subjected to gratuitous defamation and hostile interrogation in the quality media, academia and race-relations bureaucracy. The national question is obscured in political culture by fallout from a continuing culture war against the historical Australian nation. Many of the premises on which ethnic policy have been based since the 1970s are simply false, from the beneficence of diversity to the white monopoly of racism and the irrelevance of race. The elite

---

[175] Buchanan, P. J. (2002). *The death of the West. How dying populations and immigrant invasions imperil our country and civilization*. New York, St. Martin's Press.

[176] *http://www.smh.com.au/news/national/race-row-professor-suspended-for-safety/2005/07/29/1122144011263.html*, accessed 1 Sept. 2012; *http://www.theage.com.au/news/national/academic-attacks-race-article-ban/2005/09/20/1126982061849.html*, accessed 1 Sept. 2012.

media and strong elements of the professoriate allow that racial hatred in Australia is the product of Anglo-Celtic society. But in the same media and even in the Commission for Race Discrimination most ethnic disparagement is aimed at "homogenised white" people.

What would correct the situation? At the minimum, analysis based on human nature needs to be injected into the study of the national question. Behavioural biology is necessary but not sufficient for that project. The conservative intellectual heritage also needs to be revived and updated for modern times to breathe compassion and affection for Anglo Australia into ethnic studies. The philosophy of Edmund Burke regarding homeland and national cohesion – that a healthy society resembles a family with obligations to generations past, present and future – is supported and signified by the discovery of ethnic kinship, the benefits of relative homogeneity and the issues raised by the political arena's expansion to the global stage.

Such reveries appear hopelessly academic when confronted with the intolerance of left intellectuals and an immigration industry that exercises undue influence on the Australian state. Initiatives by isolated academics will be inadequate to counter entrenched politicisation. Dissent exists but not many have the tenure or the stomach to suffer isolation and contumely. Lone heroics are simply not a viable strategy for young scholars seeking to build careers studying the national question without teaching lies. It will be necessary to organise.

One or more Anglo councils are needed, non-governmental organisations along the lines of other ethnic councils but oriented more towards promoting the scientific study of ethnicity and nationalism. The council should also advocate for Anglo Australians, broadly defined. An Anglo council, and ultimately a federation of Anglo councils, would defend its constituents' ethnic interests – against defamation, exploitation and demographic swamping. It would demand full representation in multicultural bodies and seek consultative access to government. It would lobby for school children to be taught the true history of the nation. It would affirm its attachment to the land of Australia. And it would insist that if any people is to be recognised in the Constitution, pride of place should be given to that which founded the nation and provided its infrastructure, political and legal systems, culture and language. Representing the core national identity and the majority of Australians, such a council should adopt a conciliatory role to smooth ethnic relations but in a manner compatible with defending its constituents' rights and legitimate interests. The effect would be to democratise multiculturalism and the immigration industry by giving the majority of Australians representation in those spheres for the first time.

The handful of existing Anglo-Australian associations mostly promote culture and the English language, including the Britain-Australia Society and the English Speaking Union. The body that most closely approximates an ethnic agency is the British Australian Community, a small service organisation originally established to provide assistance to British immigrants.[177]

The rise of a powerful Anglo-Australian lobby would acknowledge the partial separation of nation and state. The latter would be treated as it is conceived in classical liberal theory – a Leviathan of incomparable power that can be hijacked by hostile forces. In a diverse world of self-serving elites, the state inevitably develops agendas that sometimes

---

[177] *http://britishaustraliancommunity.com/*, accessed 1 Sept. 2012. While the BAC still bears the expat stamp, it has broadened its mission to include fighting defamation and promoting awareness of the British contribution to Australia. The organisation is small, confined mainly to Melbourne and Adelaide, and is marginal to the multicultural industry. It does not have the ear of government.

conflict with the national interest. That happened in Australia from the 1960s. The case can be made that the nation needs its own institutions, a national lobby that represents its constituent's ethnic interests. Such a national whip would defend Anglo-Australia's interests against a political class that has been squandering those interests for decades. That is one, perhaps the only, way, to retain the benefits of the nation state in an era of mass migration and a self-serving elites.

Misguided Advocates of Open Borders

The poor quality of analysis behind Australia's abandonment of traditional assimilationist immigration policy reached its apotheosis recently in a spate of articles by well placed commentators. The proposal of the moment was open borders, immigration unrestricted by consideration of all factors save for security. Most Australians will reject the proposal as absurd. Unfortunately the analytical basis for policies followed by federal governments since the 1970s has not much differed apart from economic criteria. Prof. Mirko Bagaric (*SMH*, 7 April 2010, p. 15[178]), professor of law at Deakin University, argues for unrestricted immigration from the poorest to the richest countries as the best means to reduce Third World poverty. Initially his article came as a pleasant surprise to one who applies biological concepts and methods to the study of human society. Prof. Bagaric opened by stating two truths about human ethnocentrism: "[M]ost still prefer people of their own type and find different cultures jarring"; and "It is in the human DNA." [179]

However from that point the article provided almost no hint that humans are an evolved species with an interest in survival.

---

[178] http://www.smh.com.au/opinion/politics/migration-can-end-worldwide-poverty-20100406-rpaf.html

[179] Salter, F. K. (2008). "Evolutionary analyses of ethnic solidarity: An overview." *People and Place* 16(2): 15-25.

Prof. Bagaric superficially discusses three interests that could be affected by open borders – material prosperity, national security, and cultural tradition – more of which later. This leaves many interests unmentioned.

Unrestricted migration would harm Australia's national interests in ways documented by scholars in economics, sociology and related disciplines. Much of the harm is predictable from what is known about the dysfunctions of diversity. They include growing inequality in the especially invidious form of ethnic stratification. No one likes to be ruled over by a different ethnic group or to see his own people worse off than others. The result is resentment or contempt, depending on the perspective taken.

Diversity has also been associated with reduced democracy, slowed economic growth, falling social cohesion and foreign aid, as well as rising corruption and risk of civil conflict.[180]

The loss of social cohesion bears emphasis. Disapproving of birds flocking together is beside the point; it is a biological fact that needs to be taken into account.[181] Rising diversity within human societies tends to drive people apart, causing them to take sanctuary in individual pursuits and ethnic communities.

---

[180]   Re. corruption and growth: Mauro, P. (1995). "Corruption and growth." *Quarterly Journal of Economics* 110(3): 681—712.
Re. economic growth: Alesina, A., R. Baqir, et al. (1999). "Public goods and ethnic divisions." *Quarterly Journal of Economics* 114(November): 1243—1284.
Easterly, W. and R. Levine (1997). "Africa's growth tragedy: Policies and ethnic divisions." *Quarterly Journal of Economics* 112(November): 1203—1250.
Re. foreign aid: Masters, W. and M. McMillan (2004). Ethnolinguistic diversity, government, and growth. *Welfare, ethnicity, and altruism. New data and evolutionary theory*. F. K. Salter. London, Frank Cass: 123-147.
For overview see: Salter, F. K. (2004). Ethnic diversity, foreign aid, economic growth, social stability, and population policy: A perspective on W. Masters and M. McMillan's findings. *Welfare, ethnicity, and altruism. New data and evolutionary theory*. F. K. Salter. London, Frank Cass: 148-171.

[181]   McPherson, M., L. Smith-Lovin, et al. (2001). Birds of a feather: Homophily in social networks. *Annual Review of Sociology*. K. S. Cook and J. Hagan. Palo Alto, California, Annual Review. 27: 415-444.

The practical consequences are reduced public altruism or social capital, evident in falling volunteerism, government welfare for the aged and sick, public health care[182] and a general loss of trust.[183] Ethnic diversity is second only to lack of democracy in predicting civil war.[184] Globally it correlates negatively with governmental efficiency and prosperity.[185]

Thus the thrust of accumulating research in several disciplines indicates that unrestricted mass immigration would be disastrous for wealthy countries. Some of this research has been well publicised; some has been published in Australia.

There are also philosophical issues that deserve comment.

I found the single-minded concern with Third World poverty puzzling, especially coming from a declared moral universalist. It is true that poverty would be reduced for those immigrating to the wealthy West, but do not the populations of industrial countries also have interests – in ecological sustainability and national continuity – that would be injured by the influx of millions of foreigners? Should not global problems be solved in ways that optimize interests instead of benefiting one

---

[182] Sanderson, S. and T. Vanhanen (2004). Reconciling the differences between Sanderson's and Vanhanen's results. *Welfare, ethnicity, and altruism. New data and evolutionary theory*. F. K. Salter. London, Frank Cass: 119-120.

[183] Salter, F. K., Ed. (2002). *Risky transactions. Trust, kinship, and ethnicity*. Oxford and New York, Berghahn.
Salter, F. K., Ed. (2004). Welfare, ethnicity, & altruism: New data & evolutionary theory. London, Frank Cass.
Leigh, A. (2006). "Trust, inequality and ethnic heterogeneity." *The Economic Record* 82(258): 268-280.
Putnam, R. D. (2007). "*E Pluribus Unum*: Diversity and community in the twenty-first century. The 2006 Johan Skytte Prize lecture." *Scandinavian Political Studies* 30: 137-174.
Healy, E. (2007). "Ethnic diversity and social cohesion in Melbourne." *People and Place* 15(4): 49-64.

[184] Rummel, R. J. (1997). "Is collective violence correlated with social pluralism?" *Journal of Peace Research* 34(3): 163—176.

[185] Alesina, A. and E. Spolaore (2003). *The size of nations*. Cambridge, MA, MIT Press.

population at the expense of another? Should we not be aiming at win-win outcomes?

From the global perspective, humanity as a whole stands to lose from overpopulation. As the late Garrett Hardin pointed out, allowing poor countries, which generally have high birth rates, the expedient of offloading excess population on low-birth rate regions reduces the incentive to solve their own population problem, for example by tackling the poverty and under-education of women. Global overpopulation can only be solved one country at a time, not by rewarding profligacy.

Another philosophical issue is Prof. Bagaric's equating parochialism with morally repugnant "racism". Surely that is not true, firstly because "racism" has no agreed definition and has been deployed for ideological and ad hominem purposes. It is more an instrument of abuse than of reason. If its use cannot be avoided it should be reserved to describe ethnically aggressive statements and acts, not the peaceful expression of pro-social sentiments common to humans everywhere.

Secondly, the notion that preference for one's own people is immoral ignores the universal interest we all share in particular affiliations. All humans share parochial interests that give rise to social preferences. It would be maladaptive not to prefer people of our own type, beginning with kin. And in general this preference is moral. Bearing and caring for our own children, choosing friends on intuition, and having a special affection for our own country cannot be equated with hating others.[186] A liberal society that allows free expression of these moderate preferences is hardly the moral inferior of one in which the elite scolds and punishes the people's aspirations to have a country of their own.

---

[186] Cashdan, E. (2001). "Ethnocentrism and xenophobia: A cross-cultural study." *Current Anthropology* 42(5): 760 - 765.

The universality of parochial interests contradicts Prof. Bagaric when he states: "For most of human history there have been few migration limits. . . . A relevant reason [for restricting immigration] cannot be a person's birthplace. This is merely a happy or unhappy coincidence." The anthropological reality is the precise opposite: until recent decades almost all human societies have sought to prevent permanent mass migration. Western societies since about 1965 are rare exceptions. Hunter gatherers and primitive agriculturalists, farmers and herders have all laid claim to a territory and fiercely defended it. Marriage partners have been found almost exclusively within the ethnic group, encompassing the local dialect. The psychological motivations for this are well established in such predispositions as social identity mechanisms, collectivism, assortment by similarity, innate cognition of human kinds, and rational choice.[187] Evolutionary origins of territoriality and ethnocentrism are indicated by their being human universals as well as being found in apes. And from the evolutionary perspective, which acknowledges the limited carrying capacity of all territories and of the world itself, it is maladaptive to allow one's lineage – family, clan, or ethnic group – to be replaced by others.[188]

The vital interest all societies have in controlling a territory also falsifies the assertion that national security consists solely of defending individual citizens from attack, for example by vetting immigrants for terrorist connections as is already the practice with tourists. Unlike tourists, immigrants affect the receiving country's numbers, identity and cohesion. Societies thus have a corporate interest in retaining national sovereignty, which entails control of a territory. This helps explain the historical pattern of corporate liberty being put before citizen's

---

[187] MacDonald, K. (2001). "An integrative evolutionary perspective on ethnicity." *Politics and the Life Sciences* 20(1): 67-79.

[188] Salter, F. K. (2002). "Estimating ethnic genetic interests: Is it adaptive to resist replacement migration?" *Population and Environment* 24(2): 111—140.

rights.[189] Inviting the world to a country as prosperous as Australia would result in the displacement of the Australian people inside their historical homeland. This is an outcome even more maladaptive than enslavement because it would be permanent.

The final philosophical point I shall discuss is the claim that open borders are somehow consistent with liberal thinking because everyone in the world has the same rights. The problem with arguing from rights is that they can conflict, as implicitly admitted in the disclaimer that no one should infringe on others' rights. Arguments based on interests have the same problem, but also the advantage of undercutting a mountain of abstractions. Interests are more readily prioritised in accordance with knowledge of biology and society. John Stuart Mill, the father of modern liberalism, though generally a universalist, was sufficiently acquainted with human nature and the real world to support the national principle:

> *Where the sentiment of nationality exists in any force, there is a prima facie case for uniting all the members of the nationality under the same government, and a government to themselves apart . . . One hardly knows what any division of the human race should be free to do if not to determine with which of the various collective bodies they choose to associate themselves.*[190]

Mill also wrote:

> *Free institutions are next to impossible in a country made up of different nationalities. Among people*

---

[189] Skinner, Q. (1998). *Liberty before liberalism.* Cambridge, Cambridge University Press.

[190] Mill, J. S. (1960). Chapter XVI: On nationality. *Representative government. Three essays by John Stuart Mill.* J. S. Mill. London, Oxford University Press: 380—388, p. 381.

> *without fellow-feeling, especially if they read and*
> *speak different languages, the united public opinion,*
> *necessary to the working of representative*
> *government, cannot exist.*[191]

Mill is not the final word on these subjects but he does show
that basing an argument on rights does not logically entail open
borders.

The poor calibre of open-borders arguments raises questions.
How could the research documented above be ignored – not
even hinted at – by a professional academic in the internet age?
Individual scholars are technically responsible for covering the
literature bearing on their research. But in this case there is the
mitigating circumstance of the general state of the social
sciences in Australia and overseas. A month after Prof. Bagaric's
article appeared I have not come across one academic rebuttal.
The *SMH* has not published a reply by another professor
pointing out the obvious empirical fallacies, the failures of
scholarship, the sloppy and inflammatory language. Neither has
there been a storm of denunciation by colleagues or the media;
no multiply-signed letters sent to newspapers defending the
credibility of Deakin University or the humanities and social
sciences. No meetings of academics and students calling for an
explanation. Nothing on radio or television. The online
comments were generally critical and cogent but none of these
authors identified as an academic. It seems that ordinary
citizens have retained their common sense, while intellectuals
are ominously silent.

Mike Steketee, a senior commentator at *The Australian*
newspaper (10 April 2010[192]), appears to disagree with Bagaric.

---

[191]   Ibid., p. 382.

[192]   *http://www.theaustralian.com.au/politics/opinion/open-borders-a-well-meant-
road-to-chaos/story-e6frgd0x-1225851739011*

He also takes issue with Chris Berg,[193] a research fellow at the Institute for Public Affairs who also proposes unrestricted immigration. Steketee writes that advocating open borders is "well intentioned" but would cause "chaos", without describing the latter state. Well intentioned? He agrees with Bagaric and Berg that opening the floodgates would be ethical and that it would reduce Third World poverty. It would be the liberal thing to do in light of universal human rights: "[W]e believe individuals have the same rights, wherever they live". But alas democracy would get in the way. Voters would reject the dissolution of the nation state and the installation of a world government. They continue to support (immoral) tough treatment of boat people. Mr. Steketee thinks that despite the proven benefits of immigration the Australian people wish to retain "control of their destiny", implying that a rational electorate would let go and accept a much larger immigrant intake.

It seems that Mr. Steketee cannot fault Prof. Bagaric or Mr. Berg on social or ethical grounds. Indeed, he agrees that the free movement of people across borders is ideal. His disagreement, such as it is, concerns public relations and the pace of transformation that is politically feasible. Let us then examine Mr. Berg's argument.

Berg's article strikes a radical libertarian stance that also fails to acknowledge collective interests. Instead he focuses on moral claims, namely that all humans have equal moral worth regardless of where they live (p. 1). He also emphasises the benefits of immigration to immigrants. The following provides the gist of the remainder of his argument:

> But immigration is good for the developed world, too. It's good for the economy—immigrants end up being entrepreneurs and shopkeepers; employees and

---

[193] Berg, C. (2010). "Open the borders." *Policy* **26**(1): 3-7.

employers; and consumers and producers. More
people mean more creativity, more opportunity, and
more culture. Migrants bring skills, knowledge and
international connections (p. 3).

As Mr. Berg does not distinguish immigrants by education or
origins, every sentence of the above quote is either outright
false or contentious according to available research. Immigrants
from impoverished countries do not provide overall benefits to
advanced economies, though they help some employers by
reducing wages.[194] Inequality rises. In the United States Third
World immigration increases the size of the overall economy
but reduces per capita incomes. It is the latter that affects living
standards. Immigrants from different cultures differ
dramatically in their educational performance and
entrepreneurship for several generations.

Prof. Bagaric writes off the nation as essentially racist. Mr. Berg
thinks that "[t]here's really nothing that special about national
borders or the nation itself." This is a strong claim but it
becomes clear that Mr. Berg thinks that a nation is a state,
failing to make an elementary and important distinction.[195] A
nation is at its core an ethnic group living in its homeland, with
shared elements of culture and means of communication. A
nation can exist without its own state, an example being the
Kurds. And most states contain more than one nation.
Examples include empires and the products of colonial
cartography such as Iraq and most of sub-Sahara Africa. All
nation states are built around a founding ethnic core.[196]
However even without this distinction Mr. Berg is wise to state

---

[194]   Borjas, G. J. (2004). "Increasing the supply of labor through immigration:
Measuring the impact on native-born workers." *Center for Immigration Studies
Backgrounder. http://www.hks.harvard.edu/fs/gborjas/Papers/cis504.pdf*

[195]   Connor, W. (1978). "A nation is a nation, is a state, is an ethnic group, is a . . ."
Ethnic and Racial Studies **1**(4): 378-400.

[196]   Smith, A. D. (1986). *The ethnic origins of nations*. Oxford, Basil Blackwell.

that: "A nation is the most convenient mechanism by which the institutions of liberty can be delivered." (p. 4) True enough, but is that not a good reason for libertarians and all who treasure civil rights to defend national integrity?

The intellectual void surrounding the concept of the nation becomes most apparent when Mr. Berg wonders why an otherwise consistent libertarian, Murray Rothbard, thought that culture is worth defending by restricting immigration (p. 6). He quotes Rothbard's reason thus: "[A]s the Soviet Union collapsed, it became clear that ethnic Russians had been encouraged to flood into Estonia and Latvia in order to destroy the cultures and languages of these peoples." Not a bad reason. It could be supported by other examples of regimes that have used the demographic weapon attempting to swamp patriotic resistance, such as China in Tibet, Indonesia in West Irian or the Blair Labour government in Britain.[197] The extraordinary thing is that Mr. Berg offers no comment after quoting Rothbard. It is as if the concepts being used, "ethnic" and "culture and languages" failed to register. But they are realities that affect society on a massive scale. Australian policy makers should bear in mind that ethnic nationalism is still a powerful force that tears countries and empires apart and creates new nations. Recent examples are the dismemberment of the Soviet and Yugoslavian empires in the 1990s. When people are allowed to choose they vote for policies that make or keep them as the ethnic majority. The result is that spreading democracy creates relatively homogeneous small states with heightened social capital and its flip side of social stability, efficient government, low corruption, more democracy, and higher economic growth.[198] Why would a libertarian want open

---

[197] Whitehead, T. (2009). Labour wanted mass immigration to make UK more multicultural, says former adviser. *The Telegraph*. London.
   http://www.telegraph.co.uk/news/uknews/law-and-order/6418456/Labour-wanted-mass-immigration-to-make-UK-more-multicultural-says-former-adviser.html

borders? Why would anyone want to become a minority in his own country?

By the way, one can add to Rothbard's excellent reason for defending the cultural integrity of nations. All the benefits of relative homogeneity (and thus of assimilation and prudent immigration) documented above belong to nations, not to multi-ethnic states. Switzerland's highly decentralised structure in which the cantons resemble semi-autonomous nation states is the exception that proves the rule. The Soviets attempted to Russify Estonia and Latvia as a means of controlling those territories. They assumed that the ethnic-Russian minorities would maintain their identity distinct from that of the target nations for some time. As these national communities shrank in relative size they were meant to become just another competing ethnic group. National unity would be replaced by a multi-ethnic state, and the capacity of the original Estonian and Latvian nations to strategise on their own behalves would be diminished. This is what Rothbard was getting at. And who would put it past the Soviets to have reckoned that if demographic transformation could be continued long enough, the original nation would die. Another might arise in its place but that would take a long time and would not replace what was lost to the original nation.

Combined with the lack of critical response to the Bagaric article, these two pieces, one by a senior press commentator, the other by a researcher with a respected think tank, confirm the impression that the egregious standard of analysis behind open borders advocacy is not aberrant but common at the elite level of Australian political culture. The problem lies with an influential tradition well established within the universities and intellectual class as a whole.

---

[198]   Alesina, A. and R. Wacziarg (1998). Little countries: Small but perfectly formed. *The Economist*: 63-65.

How have so many scholars come to ignore accessible knowledge about human nature and society bearing on issues of immigration and ethnicity? Australia's 39 universities employ thousands of lecturers and professors in relevant disciplines. Any one of them should be able to expose elements of the case for open borders. A first year student of social anthropology should know that borders have always been closed to replacement-level migration. Students of government and sociology should know in outline both sides of the diversity debate. How can bold assertions such as those in the three articles examined here go unremarked? What is being taught at our universities?

A century ago the social sciences began suing for divorce from the biological sciences.[199] Reconciliation began in the 1970s but sociology, political science, large sections of anthropology and much of the humanities remain aloof. Add to that the political straight jacketing of these fields, an important reason for their doctrinaire rejection of inconvenient scholarship and biology alike, and it is not surprising that we see utopian socialism of the most naive variety emanating unchallenged from the professoriate.

The evidence refuting the case for open borders also applies to the scale and diversity of existing immigration policy. Any policy is suspect that threatens a country's ecological sustainability, increases diversity or tends to subordinate the core ethnic group. Such a trend was already in place for many years before historian Geoffrey Blainey warned that immigration from non-traditional Asian source countries was outrunning its welcome in the mid 1980s.[200]

---

[199] Degler, C. (1991). In search of human nature: The decline and revival of Darwinism in American social thought. Oxford, Oxford University Press.

[200] Blainey, G. (1984). *All for Australia*. North Ryde, Australia, Methuen Haynes.

Continuing high level of immigration, let alone open borders, are endangering the sustainability Australia's First World living standards. We are burning up our ecological capital. The only population difference between the immigration levels adopted by succeeding governments over recent decades and open borders is the date at which the country becomes overcrowded. In addition ethnic stratification is growing. Most Aboriginal Australians remain an economic underclass and some immigrant communities show high levels of long-term unemployment. Anglo Australians, still about 70 percent of the population, are presently being displaced disproportionately in the professions and in senior managerial positions by Asian immigrants and their children.[201] The situation is dramatic at selective schools which are the high road to university. Ethnocentrism is not a White syndrome and it is not surprising that immigrant communities harbour invidious attitude towards Anglo Australians, disparaging their culture and the legitimacy of their central place in national identity.[202]

The democratic process has been prevented from correcting our maladaptive immigration policies due to bipartisanship – a long-term deal between the major political parties to keep immigration issues off the table at election time. The collusion began responsibly enough as a measure to facilitate assimilation during the massive post-WWII immigration program from Europe. By the 1970s bipartisanship served to shield both parties from majority objections while they profited from multicultural politics, garnering votes from immigrant communities in exchange for immigration favours. Arguably this collusion would have been difficult to sustain if a

---

[201] Wilkinson, P. (2007). The Howard legacy: Displacement of traditional Australia from the professional and managerial classes. Essendon, Australia, Independent Australian Publishers.

[202] Zevallos, Z. (2005). "'It's like we're their culture': Second-generation migrant women discuss Australian culture." *People and Place* 13(2): 41-49.

substantial number of academics and commentators had spoken truth to power.

Instead, the rapid transformation of Australia by mass Third World immigration has been a top-down revolution in which politicised circles within academia have been complicit. Political leaders and citizens alike look to intellectuals for the facts and analysis needed to make wise policy. In technical matters we have been well served, but not with regard to issues of population and diversity. The policy failure is not limited to the present federal government. It goes back decades, as does the failure of the nation's brain trust. Correction will necessitate tackling the intellectual and ideological corruption of the humanities and social sciences by greatly increasing intellectual diversity and free speech within the universities and the ABC. For the world of ideas is one arena in which diversity is an unalloyed benefit, where imposed homogeneity demonstrably degrades standards.

Hiram Caton: Australian Pioneer of Biosocial Science

What leads some scholars to question the humanities and social sciences' pervasive rejection of biology? What are the consequences when they do? This article attempts to answer these questions in the case of one individual, the late distinguished academic Hiram Caton (1936-2010). His efforts to introduce biobehavioural factors into historiography and political analysis had limited impact, especially in Australia, and brought him into conflict with colleagues. As described below, he believed the resistance was due in part to unscientific motives, including utopianism and intolerance on the political left.

Hiram Caton was a philosopher, historian and political scientist who made the interface between the social sciences and the life sciences – what he termed "biosocial science" – a major theme of his research. He was a founding member of the American-based Association for Politics and the Life Sciences and from 1994 was a fellow of the Australian Institute of Biology. In this essay I seek to identify the intellectual and personal experiences that led him to adopt and persist with biosocial science despite the costs of reduced funding, isolation and, on occasion, intellectual affray (though he did not always consider that a cost).

Hiram Caton was born in North Carolina in 1936 to Baptist parents. In his youth he showed scholarly ability. Bored with Southern culture he sought exotic experiences by joining the Army in order to serve in Europe. He performed military service in Germany from the mid 1950s where he met Theodore Adorno, leader of the Frankfurt School. The meeting occurred because Caton had been appointed to help establish the 3rd Armored Division Historical Society, though his main job was as Division journalist.[203] He entered Chicago University as an undergraduate in 1960 where, like future colleague Roger Masters, he was influenced by Leo Strauss, one of a group of Jewish scholars who had fled Nazi Germany. Caton adopted Strauss's intellectual mission to "comprehend the track of modern thought". He was also attracted by Strauss's criticism of American political science that it had rejected political philosophy.

Strauss's influence is confirmed by several publications by Caton both popular and scholarly. In 1969 he reviewed one of Strauss's books for the conservative readership of *National Review*.[204] Caton wrote a memorial article, "Der hermeneutische Weg Leo Strauss" (The Hermeneutical Approach of Leo Strauss) after Strauss's death.[205] He is recognised as one of Strauss's students who, like Masters, was inspired by his teacher and achieved prominence in his field.[206] Though Caton continued to esteem Strauss, he abandoned his

---

[203] *http://hiram-caton.com/pages/hiramkey.php*, accessed 16 Feb. 2011.

[204] *National Review* 25 Feb. 1969, 21/7, pp. 181-2.

[205] University of Chicago Library, Leo Strauss Papers, Series IV, Subseries 3, Box 27, Folder 8, 1973 or 1974;
http://ead.lib.uchicago.edu/learn_on3.php?eadid=ICU.SPCL.STRAUSSLEO &format=raw-xml&collection=project/SCRC&q=strauss, accessed April 2011.

[206] Catherine Zuckert and Michael Zuckert (2006). *The truth about Leo Strauss: Political philosophy and American democracy*. Chicago, University of Chicago Press, p. 29.

agenda in the 1970s, a development accelerated by the new scholarship on Machiavelli by J. G. A. Pocock.

While at Chicago, he took a major in Arabic language and civilisation, a course of study he extended in a masters degree. Subsequently he also learned French and German sufficiently to conduct research in those languages. On the advice of his Islamic philosophy teacher and Strauss, Caton then undertook a year of philosophy in Freiburg among Martin Heidegger's circle, under the latter's student Heribert Boeder. Next stop was Yale, where he was awarded his doctorate on Descartes in 1966. A teaching position at Bucknell College was soon followed in 1967 by a position in the philosophy department at Penn State University where he enjoyed a productive interaction with Stanley Rosen, another Straussian. It was at Penn State that he wrote the book on Descartes, *The Origin of Subjectivity*[207] and developed a fascination with child behaviour, anticipating his later introduction to human ethology. Also while at Penn State the eruption of militant student protests drew him reluctantly into political action. He joined and soon led a faculty group opposed to the disruption. He also rekindled contacts with some senior editors of *National Review* and began writing for the magazine as a Straussian. This might have been seen as conservatism though in fact it was a form of liberalism that defended the university tradition and the maintenance of order and rational administration. Later Caton would classify himself as a "hard liberal". In 1965 his *National Review* circle welcomed the immigration reform legislation of that year.[208] Some traditional conservative values were to emerge later in Caton's life that many Southern Baptists would have understood—opposition to abortion, eugenics and humanism—

---

[207] Hiram P. Caton (1973). *The origin of subjectivity: An essay on Descartes*. New Haven, Yale University Press.

[208] Personal communication, 25 July 2010.

though they might have been puzzled at the absence of values related to people and place.

In 1971 Caton won a three year research fellowship offered by the Australian National University in Canberra. His research proposal was the theme of what would become, in 1988, *The Politics of Progress*. Though not the book's thesis, it contributed to biopolitics, the element of biosocial science dealing with political phenomena. In 1976 he took an appointment as foundation professor of history at the newly established Griffith University in Brisbane, where he would stay for the remainder of his career. He was often frustrated in his attempt to introduce life science perspectives into the curriculum despite his seniority in the School of Humanities and serving a term as School dean. He had some impact. Students were enthralled by the subject matter as well as the panache with which it was presented. The lessons I learnt from 1984 to 1990 as his research student, including his ethological critique of sociobiology, influenced my outlook and research agenda for many years. But usually Caton's biosocial ideas experienced a negative reception from colleagues.

Here is an appropriate place to consider the qualities that pushed Caton forward with ideas that were often frowned upon by colleagues. Intelligence is an insufficient explanation. Although an incisive analyst with an encyclopedic memory, he had mixed school results. Algebra defeated him and his SAT score was not exceptional. Character was decisive. The first quality was rugged individualism, translated intellectually into fierce independence of thought. Another was a (Southern?) rebelliousness against all attempts at intimidation. I recall him saying that as a young scholar he rebelled against intellectual authority. He remained a rebel. Another quality was verbal pugilism. Hiram Caton was an intellectual Achilles. From an early age he demonstrated not only audacity but a love of disputation. Wounds were kept private. As a boy he enjoyed the interpersonal collisions of American football that he experienced playing linebacker and was an enthusiastic spectator thereafter. He summed up this aspect of his personality by quoting an epigram:

> Oh some speak very softly, and some are most polite,
> And some will make concessions, and admit you may be right,
> But I'm for disputation, and a good old fashioned fight.

According to Wayne Hudson, a long term colleague at Griffith University,[209] Caton's combativeness was combined with certain intellectual characteristics. He was a true free-thinker with wide ranging interests who produced heterodox ideas. He was a factualist, open to making unexpected discoveries. And he had a nose for bad religions, the last being the Darwin cult (discussed below).

A final quality was the variety of liberalism described above. In my view this was an important ingredient because it contributed to the moral dimension of Caton's stand. The following example demonstrates how these qualities could combine to produce heroic autonomy.

In 1985, my second year at Griffith University, he wrote a devastating criticism of a proposed course on women's studies. His objection was that the course contradicted and would keep students ignorant of many scientifically established biological influences on gender roles. His argument was broad and rich with data drawn from behavioural endocrinology, physiology, psychology, and anthropology. The critique had no appreciable effect, a practical indicator of the reception of biosocial science. After the usual "peer" review process the course proposal was accepted unchanged. A colleague at the time and an advocate of

---

[209] Personal communication, 4 Jan. 2011.

the new course acknowledged that Caton's "sustained opposition" was the main obstacle encountered.[210] He did not consider the decision legitimate and became a whistle blower. In his own words:

> [I] hatched a scheme to expose Griffith's radical curriculum to the predominantly conservative Queensland electorate. [I] leagued with a conservative women's association, Women Who Want to Be Women, who opposed feminism; together [we] pressured Queensland's conservative government to take corrective action on 'the nation's most socialist university', as conservatives called it. [My] proposed solution: the Queensland government should sack the Griffith University Council and reconstitute it! [211]

The whistle blower was indicted for disloyalty to the university and its standards. He agreed to defend himself at a meeting open to faculty and students. Caton remained courteous in responding to the host of accusers. It should be emphasised that this stand had nothing to do with moral judgment of the life styles of some of those promoting the course. His motive was defense of the normative university. He objected to known fallacies being sold by an institution charged with seeking and teaching truth. This event showed Caton's confidence in biobehavioural science and his growing repudiation of the legitimacy of those social sciences that had sealed themselves off from it. "[T]he stimulus to the self-confident conduct of biopolitics was perhaps Hiram's most important contribution . . ." (Roger Masters[212]). Perhaps his resolve had been stiffened by

---

[210] Chilla Bullbeck (1987). "Gender studies at Griffith University." *Women's Studies International Forum* 10(5): 537-41.

[211] *http://hiram-caton.com/pages/hiramkey.php*, accessed 16 Feb. 2011.

[212] Roger Masters, personal communication, 18 Jan. 2011.

the refutation in 1983 of Margaret Mead's famous Samoan ethnography by Australian anthropologist Derek Freeman, discussed below.

The episode was a skirmish in a running battle. Caton's biosocial research had put him on a collision course with the left academic establishment. That he was well armed intellectually for the fight was demonstrated by his access to some elite institutions. He was a fellow of the National Humanities Center in North Carolina from 1982-3 while working on *The Politics of Progress*. In 1987 he was invited by E. O. Wilson to spend three months working in his department at Harvard. In 1988 he was a guest scientist at the Max Planck Research Center for Human Ethology, Andechs, Germany.

His first book, *The Origins of Subjectivity: An Essay on Descartes*, published in 1973, was not overtly a conservative manifesto, celebrating as it did the triumph of rationalism over clerical mysticism. And his interpretation of Cartesian philosophy can be viewed as lying outside the house of biosocial science, though for Caton, Descartes' thought was the antechamber of the scientific world view. It is only when compared with the irrationalism of much contemporary humanities and social studies that the scientific perspective appears orthodox. Caton was aware that, like Descartes, his advocacy of a rational view of human nature was controversial and revolutionary and invited ideologically motivated opposition. Descarte's example worked philosophically as well as inspirationally, perhaps also for Caton's vision of biopolitical science. He later summarised Descarte's "vast innovation" forged in the teeth of the Inquisition:

> *Classical and ecclesiastical learning are swept away completely. Magic, alchemy, and astrology are thrown out on their ear. The world is as perspicuous and unmysterious as a clock; comets come from outer*

space bearing no messages from Jehovah; all bones can be fractured; a human corpse is a rusting machine, nothing more; the universe is infinite (the opinion for which Bruno was burned); the planetary system is Copernican; in the whole expanse of the universe there are no miracles, not one; belief in resurrection is for the "weak-minded" while the "strong-minded" itch to master and possess nature; Scholasticism is decadence usurping the name of philosophy, which Descartes challenges to mortal combat. Such views define philosophic isolation and independence of thought: the break with received opinion is clean, sharp, radical. The past is a smoking ruin, and a new era dawns.[213]

Perhaps the most important paper written by Caton during the 1980s was "Pascal's Syndrome: Positivism as a Symptom of Depression and Mania", published in 1986.[214] The paper advanced the thesis that intellectual history is not only a matter of ideas but mood states and the psychobiology that contributes to them. One such mood state, depression, has influenced the ideas of many scholars. The analysis was radically multidisciplinary, introducing to the history of philosophy such fields as the etiology of depression and the neurology of altered states of consciousness including conversion experiences. It deployed the biogenic amine hypothesis of depression and mania. The technical content of such papers makes them subversive of left sociology. "Hiram Caton's contribution is to be *celebrated* as a gift to the advance of the scientific paradigm that will inevitably become the basis of all social science due to

---

[213] Hiram P. Caton (1988). The politics of progress: The origins and development of the commercial republic, 1600-1835. Gainesville, University of Florida Press, p. 56.

[214] Hiram P. Caton (1986). "Pascal's Syndrome: Positivism as a symptom of depression and mania." *Zygon* 21: 319-351.

the steady advances of fields like behavioral genetics and neuroscience" (Roger Masters[215]).

The book most relevant to biopolitics is *The Politics of Progress: The Origins and Development of the Commercial Republic, 1600-1835*, published in 1988. Research extended over fifteen years beginning in 1971 at the Australian National University (ANU). The scholars Caton thanked for assisting his research present an unusual mix for a work in political theory and history of ideas: not only the intellectual historian J. G. A. Pocock and political scientist Harvey C. Mansfield Jr. of Harvard's Department of Government but also S. A. Barnett of the Department of Zoology at the ANU, Derek Freeman, also at the ANU, and E. O. Wilson, head of Harvard's Museum of Comparative Zoology.[216]

The book's thesis is that the Industrial Revolution was the outcome not only of physical technologies such as the steam engine but also of social technologies, especially the emergence of prudent political management in the form of republican constitutional government, the commercial republic of the book's title. This was a cluster of social technologies developed initially in Holland, England and France that removed morality and religion from public policy and focused government on providing the universal goods of peace and liberty. It redirected private energies towards accumulating wealth through methodic, purposive work. This goes well beyond Max Weber's theory of capitalism, that it was the result of the Protestant work ethic. For one thing, it allows for the contributions of non-Protestants to rational-capitalist economics, including Ashkenazi Jews, whose economic behaviour Weber categorised as that of a pariah minority.

---

[215] Personal communication, 18 Jan. 2011.

[216] Caton, *The Politics of Progress*, pp. xi-xii.

The theory of social technology–the term in this context appears to have been invented by Caton–was a significant innovation. It distilled and clarified an idea in ethology that had been developed most clearly by the pioneer Austrian ethologist Irenaeus Eibl-Eibesfeldt, though it also occurred in philosophical mode in nineteenth century English liberal social theory. A social technology is a rule or practice that shapes and coordinates the behaviour of groups or populations by manipulating their social instincts. The theory is effectively conservative because it entails limits to social engineering and thus casts doubt on utopian and revolutionary ideas. Reintroduction of human nature reverses decades of anti-biological bias in the social sciences. Caton's use of the theory to deploy ethology, anthropology and sociobiology in historiography was largely worked out by the time of his presentation to the 1982 meeting of the American Political Science Association.[217] This was the paper that so impressed me that I undertook postgraduate studies with him in Australia instead of in the U.S. as originally planned.

Caton drew attention to the elitism of the politics of progress. Democracy was necessary to secure legitimacy but it was the professional politicians and bureaucrats who ruled in top-down fashion. This was the view of the great Whig philosopher John Locke: "The greatest part cannot know, and therefore must believe".[218] Caton translated thus: "Reason for the gentlemen who govern, faith for the multitude–this is the formula for politic religion espoused by Machiavelli and Sarpi, by the politiques of the French court, by the Erastians in Holland and England, and expounded in classic fashion by Hobbes and Spinoza". Perhaps this represented the continuing influence of Strauss, though applied to a broader set of relations between

[217] Hiram P. Caton (1982). "Biosocial science: Knowledge for enlightened political leadership." Paper presented at the American Political Science Association annual convention, Denver, Colorado, 2-6 September 1982.

[218] Locke, *Works*, 1: p. 410, quoted in Caton, *The Politics of Progress*, p. 217.

elite and people. Roger Masters, the dean of American biopolitics, thinks so.

> *Hiram dared to indicate that, for a genuine scientist, the theory of evolution by natural selection and the inclusion of Homo sapiens in the domain of natural species is genuinely "sacred". He also dared to admit that sometimes silence is needed to preserve the potential for the unfettered activities of the human intellect. Having studied the philosophic tradition illustrating this truth under Leo Strauss at the University of Chicago, I had no problem understanding why Hiram was fearless in addressing the challenge of so-called "creation scientists".*[219]

Actually Caton's scholarship was not directed at religion but at the irrationalism of the social sciences. This became clear in his contribution to the controversy surrounding Derek Freeman's[220] refutation of Margaret Mead's[221] famous doctoral thesis that Samoan adolescent sexuality is free of the drama experienced by teenagers in Western societies.[222] Apart from intrinsic interest, the Mead-Freeman controversy is important for the light it sheds on ideological bias in the social sciences, a bias that had led to the denial of knowledge about human nature. Caton thought that Freeman was too kind to Mead when he denied the role of malfeasance, though culpability must also rest on Mead's professor, Franz Boas.[223] The exposure of Mead's error kindled Caton's interest in "truth management" in

---

[219] Roger Masters, personal communication, 18 Jan. 2011.

[220] Derek Freeman (1983). *Margaret Mead and Samoa: The making and unmaking of an anthropological myth*. Canberra, Australian National University Press.

[221] Margaret Mead (1928/1961). *Coming of age in Samoa. A psychological study of primitive youth for Western civilisation*. New York, Morrow.

[222] Hiram P. Caton (1990). *The Samoa reader: Anthropologists take stock*. Lanham, MD, University Press of America.

modern science,[224] discussed further below. Like historian Carl Degler[225] he sought to understand how biological knowledge of human nature had been excluded for so long from the social sciences.[226] But the scope of his inquiry was broader. He noted that Degler failed to describe advances in IQ testing since the Second World War and the huge controversy initiated by Arthur Jensen's study of race differences. Caton also noted the omission in Degler's study of the Minnesota Twin Studies conducted by Thomas Bouchard and J. Philippe Rushton's sociobiological analysis of race differences. "Particularly grievous . . . is the want of any mention of the debate over the legacy of Margaret Mead and the Boasian paradigm instigated by Derek Freeman's 1983 refutation of Mead's most influential study."[227]

The Mead-Freeman controversy sparked Caton's interest in what he called truth management, the fraudulent presentation of science. "The fraud consists in representing a specific and contingent interpretation of evidence as if it were unalloyed truth enjoying the unanimous endorsement of the relevant cadre of scientists. Truth management, then, is wanton abuse of scientific authority".[228] The analysis encompassed the contortions used to defend Margaret Meads against Derek

---

[223] *http://4hiram.wordpress.com/2008/03/24/margaret-mead-and-samoa/*, accessed 18 Feb. 2011.

[224] Hiram P. Caton (1988). "Truth management in the sciences." Search: The Official Publication of the Australian and New Zealand Association for the Advancement of Science 19(5/6): 242-244.
The concept was further developed in: Caton, H. P. (1995). *The AIDS mirage*. Sydney, University of New South Wales Press.

[225] Carl Degler (1991). In search of human nature: The decline and revival of Darwinism in American social thought. Oxford, Oxford University Press.

[226] Hiram P. Caton (1995). "Selective witness to a century of biology and culture." *Journal of Social and Evolutionary Systems* 18(1): 103-107.

[227] Caton, "Selective witness", p. 107.

[228] Caton, "Truth management".

Freeman's criticisms, outright scientific fraud, self-serving valorisation of scientists as morally superior, shortcomings of peer review and the ubiquitousness of self deception and collusion in organisations. The final example discussed was the AIDS epidemic. Caton asserted that the scientific debate had been short-circuited by a rush to adopt a single official explanation which simplified policy making. "It is deemed to be vital that the public be indoctrinated in a single point of view and that all others be branded with epithets that intimidate and marginalise opponents. Practically, it comes down to good guys and bad guys, leaving no grey areas that critics might use to assault the citadel".[229] He noted the National Institute of Health's harsh treatment of Peter Duesberg, the distinguished virologist at UCLA Berkeley, when he criticised the HIV hypothesis for AIDS in *Science* in 1988.[230] Caton joined with Duesberg and others in criticising the HIV hypothesis and the way it had been defended, a viewpoint he elaborated in a short book, *The AIDS Mirage* in 1995. The scientific consensus is that this position is in error. It was typical of Hiram Caton that he took the risky option of staking out a claim that was not necessary to his thesis. When I put this to him he responded that he thought it "weak" not to declare a position one believes to be true. Cross-disciplinary research has its burdens and hazards that can be magnified by an excess of confidence or courage.

Much biosocial science is apolitical. Its conservative implications emerge from some empirical findings that validate traditional social arrangements and institutions. An example of an apolitical project of Caton's in the 1990s was an attempt to bibliograph the entire field of human behavioural biology. With coauthors Hans van der Dennen and myself this culminated in

---

229 Caton, "Truth management".

230 *http://4hiram.wordpress.com/2008/03/27/rethinking-aids/*, accessed 9 June 2011; and see Duesberg's account at *http://www.virusmyth.com/aids/hiv/pdlecture.htm*, accessed 9 June 2011.

the book *The Bibliography of Human Behavior* published in 1993, part of the Westport series *Bibliographies and Indexes in Anthropology*. It carried about 6,000 titles across numerous fields. The effort convinced him that the behavioural sciences had already outgrown a single volume. His most ambitious research during the 1990s was intended to be a book on crowd behaviour, which he never completed, though some papers resulted.[231]

Consistent with the theme of truth management was Caton's last research effort concerning the origins and reception of evolutionary theory. He argued that Darwin has been valorised and other contributors discounted.[232] A better title for neo-Darwinism, Caton suggested, is "neo-Mendelianism" because this recognises the central role that genetics plays in modern evolutionary theory. Natural selection is not the only driver of evolution, he maintained, and besides Darwin was not the first to describe the process. Darwinism was a theoretical tool for Caton, not a substitute for religion. His views converged to an extent on other criticisms of the cultish behaviour of some Darwinists, notably by Mary Midgley and David Stove.[233]

Caton's writings reflected the growing conflict between his biopolitics and the left establishment. He saw biopolitics as part of scientific progress. It was needed to better understand society and politics as a precondition for increasing governmental prudence. Thus the separation of the social sciences and humanities from the biological sciences was regressive and in need of reform. Like many members of the

---

[231] Hiram P. Caton (1994). "A new approach to the revolutionary crowd." *Australian Journal of Politics and History* 40: 187-202.

[232] Hiram P. Caton (2007). "Getting our history right: Six errors about Darwin and his influence." *Evolutionary Psychology www.epjournal.net* 5(1): 52-69.

[233] Midgley, M. (1985). Evolution as a religion. Strange hopes and stranger fears. London, Methuen.
Stove, D. C. (1994). *Darwinian fairytales*. Aldershot, Avebury.

founding generation of biopolitical analysts, his promotion of biopolitics was connected to his critique of mainstream social science and humanities. My first encounter with this critique was in the 1982 presentation to the APSA discussed earlier. Summarising the great strides made by the life sciences in the recent decades, Caton declared:

Homo sapiens has been sectioned, stained, and clamped under the microscope by literally hundreds of methods. This [should be] big news to social scientists struggling to nail down firm knowledge with methods they know to be defective. Indeed the track record of social science over the past eighty years is dismal. Tens of thousands of highly trained researchers have expended well in excess of $2 billion without discovering a single empirical law. In the absence of empirical laws, social scientists can neither predict events nor design effective social technologies.[234]

Caton went on to note that the social sciences have been funded in part to solve social problems in such areas as pedagogy, industrial relations, and race relations. "Yet it is difficult to think of a single piece of social engineering emanating from social scientists that has solved the targeted problem. And in some areas, notably pedagogy, everything social scientists touch seems to turn to chaos."

Such criticism is to be found frequently in Caton's work. For example, in a paper on Hobbes he remarked: "Strauss thought that the contemporary outbreak of relativism and nihilism (lately called postmodernism) were the stigmata signifying the brain death of the modern philosophical tradition."[235] He ended the paper by describing the existential crisis of the humanities burdened with impressionistic methods "in an era dominated

---

[234] Caton, "Biosocial science", p. 2.

[235] Hiram P. Caton (1994). "Is leviathan a unicorn? Varieties of Hobbes interpretations." *The Review of Politics* 56(1): 103-125, p. 107.

by the industry standards of the scientific disciplines". He issued a rallying call:

> *The choice seems to be either to throw in with popular culture and political correctness, or go to the wall. Yet there is an exciting alternative: to renew the whole enterprise on the basis of the behavioral sciences. One may even think of it humanistically as the completion of Hobbes's project for a genuine political science.*[236]

A more practical recommendation came at the end of Caton's review of Francis Fukuyama's essay "The End of History", which declared victory for liberal democracy when the Soviet Union abandoned communism. After criticising the essay's reliance on Hegel and suggesting that political elites are ill-tutored by their academic advisors, he concluded:

> *[P]olitical and social thought in the West today is in a pathetic condition as a hodge-podge of paraphilosophy, mere empiricism, and obsolete theory. The thought suggests itself that the response to the Soviet abandonment of Marxism should be in kind. Let us make a try at replacing the detritus of history that clutters our social science departments. This is easier to do than [it] may seem. You just turn off the funding spigot watering mere empiricism and obsolete theory.*[237]

This was optimistic. As Caton had experienced in his own career it is biosocial science that finds itself under ideological pressure. In 1990 he felt obliged to publicly support the Canadian

---

[236] Hiram P. Caton (1994). "A new approach to the revolutionary crowd." *Australian Journal of Politics and History* 40: 187-202, p. 125.

[237] Hiram P. Caton (1989). "Stuck in time: Fukuyama's 'The End of History'". *Quadrant* 33(12): 66-69, p. 69.

psychologist J. Philippe Rushton who was facing loss of tenure for daring to apply sociobiology to the study of race differences.[238] I believe his motives to have been philosophical, not ethnic. I knew Hiram Caton for 26 years and never heard him express hostility for any race or special sympathy for Western populations. Only late in life did he consider the implications of ethnic kinship.[239]

In later years Caton admitted that his biopolitical and biosocial ideas had not gained much traction in Australia. "I abandoned efforts to teach biobehavioural materials to buy peace with colleagues."[240] Even his university's bestowal of the Doctor of Letters for *The Politics of Progress* was less than fulsome, the recipient having to nominate himself.[241] Biopolitics has remained marginal within Australia and has not become mainstream elsewhere, even in the United States where the field has been most successful. The biopolitical counter-revolution has not occurred, though the field continues to make intellectual progress. There is not one university position dedicated to biopolitics in Australia or the U.S. Neither is the subject represented among standard political science curricula.

In his 2001 report on the Australian scene, Caton made some practical proposals for promoting biopolitics such as remaining modest, being collegial, avoiding disputation[!], and winning over students (pp. 265-6). He also recommended "playing the game". These are wise words. However his personal example recommended a different direction. He exploited biosocial

---

[238] Rushton, J. P. (1995). *Race, evolution, and behavior*. New Brunswick, NJ, Transaction Publishers.

[239] Caton, H. P. (2004). "Review: On Genetic Interests: Family, Ethny and Humanity in an Age of Mass Migration." Twin Research 7(3): 306-307.

[240] Hiram P. Caton (2001). "'Biopolitics? Never heard of it': A report from Australia", in *Evolutionary approaches in the behavioral sciences: Toward a better understanding of human nature*. S. A. Peterson and A. Somit. Amsterdam, JAI-Elsevier Science: 247-269, p. 264.

[241] The author was present in the University Council when the agenda item came up.

insights to initiate creative lines of analysis, challenged colleagues on points of fact and theory, and when he detected intellectual corruption–willful error that fell outside the bounds of scholarship–appealed to the referee in the form of government and public opinion. He did what he could to turn off the spigot.

Selective bibliography of Hiram Caton's published work on biosocial science.

Hiram Caton published over 200 articles and books. The following bibliography lists some of those related to politics and the life sciences.

(1973). *The origin of subjectivity: An essay on Descartes.* New Haven, Yale University Press. 248 pages.

(1982). "Biosocial science: Knowledge for enlightened political leadership." Paper prepared for the American Political Science Association annual convention, Denver, Colarado, 2-6 September 1982.

(1986). "Sound and shoddy sociobiology." *Behavioral and Brain Sciences* 9: 188-189.

(1986). "Pascal's Syndrome: Positivism as a symptom of depression and mania." *Zygon* 21: 319-351.

(1987). "The gender jungle [review article]." *Politics and the Life Sciences* 5(2): 273-275.

(1988). *The politics of progress: The origins and development of the commercial republic, 1600-1835.* Gainesville, University of Florida Press. 639 pages.

(1988). "Truth management in the sciences." *Search: The Official Publication of the Australian and New Zealand Association for the Advancement of Science* 19(5/6): 242-244.

(1990). *The Samoa reader: Anthropologists take stock.* Lanham, MD, University Press of America. 366 pages.

(1992). "Political thought for Epigones." *Political Theory Newsletter* 4: 179-184.

(1992). "Some social consequences of gene improvement." *Policy* 8: 29-32.

(1993). *The bibliography of human behavior*. Westport, Conn., Greenwood Press. With Frank K. Salter and Johan van der Dennen.

(1994). "Is leviathan a unicorn? Varieties of Hobbes interpretations." *The Review of Politics* 56(1): 103-125.

(1994). "A new approach to the revolutionary crowd." *Australian Journal of Politics and History* 40: 187-202.

(1983/1994). Descriptive political ethology, MS., Griffith University.

(1995). *The AIDS mirage*. Sydney, University of New South Wales Press. 62 pages.

(1995). "Selective witness to a century of biology and culture." *Journal of Social and Evolutionary Systems* 18(1): 103-107.

(1996). "Eugenics." *Dictionary of ethics, theology and society*. P. A. B. Clarke and A. Linzey. London, Routledge: 326-331.

(1997). "Darwin then and now: Cameo of an undergraduate course." *Reports of the National Center for Science Education* 17(2): 17-24.

(1998). "Reinvent yourself: Labile psychosocial identity and the lifestyle marketplace." In *Indoctrinability, ideology, and warfare: Evolutionary perspectives*. I. Eibl-Eibesfeldt and F. K. Salter. Oxford and New York, Berghahn: 325–343.

(2001). "'Biopolitics? Never heard of it': A report from Australia." In *Evolutionary approaches in the behavioral sciences: Toward a better understanding of human nature*. S. A. Peterson and A. Somit. Amsterdam, JAI-Elsevier Science: 247-269.

(2004). "Review: On Genetic Interests: Family, Ethny and Humanity in an Age of Mass Migration." *Twin Research* 7(3): 306-307.

(2006). "Evolutionary constraints on democratic nation building." *Evolutionary Psychology* 4: 142-8.

(2007). "Getting our history right: Six errors about Darwin and his influence." *Evolutionary Psychology www.epjournal.net* 5(1): 52-69.

Some of these titles are available at *www.Hiram-Caton.com.*